MATCH OF THE DAY

macdonald media publishing

First published in November 2010 by **macdonald** media publishing

22 Roxburgh Road, Paisley, PA2 0UG.

info@macdonald-media.co.uk

ISBN: 0-9553126-7-1

ISBN 13: 978-0-9553126-7-0

A CIP catalogue record for this book is available from the British Library.

Design and typesetting: Cameron Heggie.

Printed and bound by Thomson Litho, East Kilbride.

INTRODUCTION

'YOU'VE certainly hooked a tiger by the tail with that selection'. Such were the words of a St Mirren colleague when I presented my list of memorable games that St Mirren have been involved in.

I am more that conscious that in highlighting these 50 games from a catalogue of well over 3,000 league and cup matches over St Mirren's 133 year history I am treading on dangerous ground.

Such a selection will, I'm sure, lead to many a contentious argument as to the most memorable occasion.

St Mirren didn't win every one of the 50 games. I have tried to be selective and for the games that were lost - 'we wuz robbed' might be appropriate, or it was one of those games that live forever in the memory and not always for the victory.

I have tried to provide the build up to each game as opposed to just portraying the act of whacking the ball into the net, which can be a mite boring. Equally many games have a postscript.

I am deeply indebted to many people and organisations for their assistance and in this respect my sincere thanks go to Kathleen Sinclair, Garthland Print, Paisley Daily Express, David Donnelly, Paisley Central Library, Glasgow Mitchell Library, Bert Bell, Saints Programme Editor, Norrie Jamieson, Allan Picken and Alistair Miller.

However a particular vote of thanks must go to Jim Crawford whose prodigious collection of St Mirren memorabilia is inexhaustible and satisfied many a need. Thank you Jim.

The writing of such a book generates a mountain of facts, figure and statistics with every reader happy to pitch in to contest the statements that might require debate; consequently I would endorse the contents with a substantial E & OE.

I hope you will find it an interesting read. Enjoy.

Alastair MacLachlan

Alistair Miller

FOREWORD

HOW often have you said :

Were you there when ?
Did you see ?
Do you remember when ?

Should the answer be YES to any of these questions, then read on and relive many happy moments.

I was delighted when Alastair asked me to write the Foreword for this interesting book that will appeal to every St Mirren fan. It is about more than St Mirren Football Club, it highlights some of the great moments of football history involving St Mirren from April 18th 1908 to April 25th 2009.

In the present day with instant information coming at you from all directions, the mind becomes overwhelmed with sound bites on many topics - you listen and soon afterwards you forget.

You may sit down with friends, as I have done, and relive a particularly memorable game you attended - you picture yourself at the match, enjoying the thrill of the team being on top, the goals scored, joining in with the singing, voicing your opinions and after the final whistle, you can't wait for the next game. Wonderful !

I experienced many memorable games in the years I played on the left wing for St Mirren, but perhaps the most remarkable match was one of the 'Classic Games' - St Mirren, the under dogs, met Celtic in the semi-final of the 1959 Scottish Cup.

Against all the odds everything went our way. We won 4-0 and went down in history. The fans found their voices with 'When The Saints Go Marching In' echoing round Hampden Park! Indeed, we did go marching in that season, straight on to Hampden Park to win the Scottish Cup.

Nothing will ever take these memories away. If I close my eyes I can be back on the pitch at Hampden with the fans in full voice.

Alastair captures all of this and so much more in this book. Some of the players described in his previous '100 Great Saints' book also feature here, giving extra depth to this book.

This is not only a series of football reports, for each and everyone of the 'Classic Games' is a story in itself.

When I was first introduced to Alastair, I thought of him in football terms. Perhaps a centre half - tall, commanding and elegant in the mould of George Young a past captain of Rangers and Scotland or perhaps Alan Hansen of Liverpool and Scotland both of whom gave sterling service to their clubs.

Alastair achieves the same with his books for he is loyal to the Club and a true St Mirren enthusiast.

For a march down memory lane and many enjoyable recollections I strongly recommend you read this book..

Alistair Miller

Willie O'Hagan

HEART OF MIDLOTHIAN 0   ST MIRREN 3

First World War Victory Cup Final

26th April 1919

ITH the signing of the Armistice to end First World War hostilities on 11th November 1918, it was time for the Scottish football scene to revert to its normal modus operandi.

The Scottish Cup competition had been suspended during the five year period embracing the conflict, although a league programme had been up and running. Thoughts of implementing an inaugural Victory Cup competition came into being in the Spring of 1919 with Hearts and St Mirren contesting the final. The progress of both clubs is as listed, together with the names of the St Mirren scorers.

St Mirren

1st Round	Dumbarton	H	0-0	
Replay	Dumbarton	A	1-0	Hodges
2nd Round	Clyde	H	3-2	Clark (2) and Thomson

| 3rd Round | Celtic | H | 1-0 | Thomson |
| Semi Final | Hibernian | A | 3-1 | Thomson (2) and Clark |

Hearts

1st Round	Bye		
2nd Round	Third Lanark	A	2-1
3rd Round	Partick Thistle	A	2-0
Semi Final	Airdrieonians	H	7-1

Some might label St Mirren as lacking in the finer subtleties of silky soccer, but if the skill factors might not have been top drawer there was certainly nothing wrong with their stamina and fitness.

Extra time had been the norm in the 1st Round tie against Dumbarton at Love Street to be followed by further extra time forays in the games with Celtic and Hibernian.

The location of this final was intriguing.

Scotland were due to meet England on international duty the following Saturday 3rd May. Ticket prices, incidentally, were rated at 10/- for the centre stand, which included admission and entertainment tax, while the east and west stands cost 7/6 and 5/-.

It would appear that the SFA authorities wanted Hampden to be in pristine condition for the Auld Enemy clash and so this Victory Cup Final was shoved sideways onto Celtic Park.

With Hearts being the pre-match favourites due to their higher position in the league, the Tynecastle club launched straight at Saints.

That attack was pretty ferocious in the early play, but fortunately they bred their goalkeepers tough in these days.

The St Mirren custodian, Donegal-born Willie O'Hagan, had to call on all his undoubted physique as the Hearts centre forward Wilson hurled himself at the big keeper in a body challenge hoping the Saints number one might drop the ball.

Hearts continued to play a quick firebrand of attacking football and as such O'Hagan was regularly on the hop. One fierce drive from Mercer saw the goalkeeper save at full stretch after John Fulton had been penalised for illegally stopping Sinclair in full flight.

The Tynecastle team were becoming frustrated.Their semi final tie against Airdrie had brought a goal every 12 minutes. Here they were up against a resolute Paisley defence in which Jock Marshall and Fulton were outstanding.

The first half finished goal-less, but Saints' Tom Page was on target immediately on the resumption, forcing keeper Black to parry his drive for a corner with Hedges making an absolute mess with the resultant flag kick.

Midway through the second half the Hearts 'Clan Wilson' threesome produced a co-ordinated move, which threatened, the Saints goal, but the combined full back efforts of Marshall and Fulton kept the Buddies goal intact.

St Mirren, however, did have the ball in the net.

Frank Hodges let fly with a drive from well out, Black saved only for Page to pounce with predatory instincts to prod the loose ball home, but referee Hamilton decreed the strike was offside.

The score sheet was still blank after the full 90 minutes and so to extra time.

Indeed, this was the fourth occasion that St Mirren had to play extra time in this competition.

It became apparent that Hearts had literally shot their bolt in their attacking ploys and the fitter Paisley men fully benefited from their training techniques and soon gained the upper hand.

Charlie Sutherland headed them into the lead and Frank Hodges made it 2-0. Then Sutherland went on to seal the win by converting a pass from Hodges.

St Mirren had won a major trophy for the first time.

However, there was a degree of confusion at the presentation ceremony. The official Victory Cup wasn't available, so the SFA authorities had to dredge out a huge shield from their cellars, which had originally been won by a Celtic youth team. Both the cup and the shield are now in safe custody at St Mirren Park.

MATCH OF THE DAY

Teams:

Hearts: *Black, Squirrelly, J. Wilson, Preston, Mercer, Sharp, Sinclair, Miller, A. Wilson, McCullough and W. Wilson.*

St Mirren: *O'Hagan, Marshall, Fulton, Perry, McKenzie, Anderson, Hodges, Page, Clark, Sutherland and Thomson.*

Referee: *G.W. Hamilton.*

Attendance: *70,000.*

MATCH OF THE DAY

Dunky Walker

ST MIRREN 2 NOTTS COUNTY 1

Barcelona Stadium Inauguration Match
22nd May 1922

HE 1921-22 season hadn't been particularly memorable. Saints had reached the 4th Round of the Scottish Cup, losing out to Rangers after a replay while, on League terms, finishing on the eighth rung of a 22 team Division One ladder was seemingly considered, in educational terms, as 'Satisfactory, must do better'.

The satisfaction factor prompted manager John Cochrane to organise an end of season tour to take in the soccer delights of the Catalonian region of Spain.

No package holiday deals in these days.

The Saints party left Glasgow Central Station on Tuesday 16th May at 10.30 pm, the itinerary taking in London, Dover, Calais, Paris and arriving in Barcelona on the Thursday.

Tired? You bet they were.

10

There had been some initial thoughts about a possible game in Paris, but the extensive terrestrial travel conditions soon negated that option. However, they did manage a couple of games against local opposition narrowly losing both.

The Paisley party was royally entertained by the Scots colony in the St Andrews District of Barcelona and enjoyed a series of sight-seeing trips allied to some sailing, regularly topped up with numerous banquets.

While the tour was essentially a winding down operation after a hard domestic season, the showpiece was a match against Notts County to herald the opening of the Del Nou Camp De Joc, Barcelona's brand new stadium, the forerunner of the now famous Nou Camp Stadium.

The cost of the Spanish champions' magnificent new edifice was the princely sum of £75,000 - a veritable fortune in the early 1920s.

It was perhaps appropriate that the Spanish invitations had been issued to St Mirren and Notts County.

The Meadow Lane outfit are the oldest English League club, their birth certificate being date stamped in 1862 - 15 years prior to St Mirren arriving on the soccer spectrum. It is also significant that both clubs were founder members of their respective national leagues.

While the Barcelona ground was essentially a magnificent piece of football architecture, St Mirren were less sure regarding the quality of the pitch.

With ambient temperatures forever in and around the 30 degrees Celsius mark, the playing surface was sun-baked with the likelihood of normal boot studs causing a clutch of blisters.

Far distant thoughts and appreciation of the famed Love Street grassy sward sprung to mind.

Played in sweltering conditions, strength-sapping touchline runs were limited in the extreme and it wasn't surprising to find a 0-0 half time scoreline.

It was hereabouts that St Mirren played their smart card.

While the English team left the field seeking a cooler environment in the dressing rooms, St Mirren opted to stay on the pitch in the baking heat.

The locals appreciated the Scottish bravado and the 20,000 partisan crowd then offered its total support to the Saints.

It wasn't until the 55th minute that St Mirren made the breakthrough, with a pinpoint cross being bulleted into the net by the goal-grabbing machine that was Dunky Walker.

It looked like the trophy that was up for grabs was heading for Paisley when, just five minutes from time, keeper Jock Bradford spilled a cross and fumbled a County shot over the line for the equaliser.

Baking heat or not, it was a trophy match with the obligatory needs of extra time and possibly even corners to count if a decision hadn't been reached.

It was the mercurial Walker who banished any thoughts of a corner count when, just five minutes from the end of extra time, he collected a ball just eight yards from goal then pirouetted on the proverbial sixpence to turn and smash home the winner.

The President of Barcelona, Juan Gamper, duly came onto the pitch to present the cup to the winning skipper Robert Birrell.

Typical cup celebrations then followed with the cup on show on the return bus trip to the team hotel with cheering crowds en route.

A sumptuous evening banquet was instrumental in cementing the new found firm relationship between Barcelona, St Mirren and Notts County.

The trophy was initially known as the Landome Cup, but engraved on the silverware is the name 'The Barcelona Cup' which in 1922 was valued at 50 Guineas.

The cup is a priceless piece of St Mirren history and many Black and White supporters are happy to pronounce that this is the first European trophy ever to be won by a British team.

Teams:

St Mirren: *Bradford, Hamilton, Birrell (Capt), Clunas, Duff, Leslie, Lawson, Gillies, Walker, Stevenson and Thomson.*

Notts County: *Streets, Ashurst, Cope, Gibson, Dinsdale, Kemp, Platts, Cook, Marriott, McPherson and Death.*

Jock Bradford

CELTIC 0 ST MIRREN 2

Scottish Cup Final

10th April 1926

HE pre-match hype surrounding this game had conjured up a wealth of statistics.

This was the 48th Scottish Cup to be contested since 1873-74, the competition being suspended during the First World War years.

Celtic were out in front in terms of being outright winners having taken the trophy on 11 occasions - one more than Queen's Park.

Equally, this final gave Celtic the opportunity to again win the double - league and cup - a feat no other club had ever achieved.

One new record was established which saw the match attendance reach new heights with 98,620 paying customers spinning through the turnstiles.

The preceding Saturday saw St Mirren entertain St Johnstone on Division One business at Love Street, the Buddies winning 3-1 and consolidating their fourth place position behind Celtic, Airdrie and Hearts.

Admission to the St Johnstone game was adults 1/- (5p in today's currency) with boys being rated at 6d. Kick off time was 3.30pm.

Celtic had a more extensive programme. After drawing 0-0 with Kilmarnock on that same Saturday, they had to fulfil a rearranged match on the following Monday, again posting a 0-0 draw, this time with Partick Thistle at Firhill.

Around the start of the cup final week top of the La Scala cinema bill in Paisley saw Charlie Chaplain featuring in 'The Gold Rush.'

The title could not have been more appropriate as the mad rush to secure a stand ticket, plus arranging transportation to Hampden Park, had to be negotiated.

A total of 1,000 stand seats had been allocated to the St Mirren fans and, clearly, this in no way satisfied the demand - they were sold out after an hour.

Ten special trains ran from Paisley's Gilmour Street to Mount Florida, but a problem on the Cathcart Circle line delayed many of the Paisley punters arriving in time.

They took matters into their own hands with a mass evacuation from the railway carriages and a scramble up the embankments to try and reach the ground in time

St Mirren were expected to field the same team that had put paid to the cup aspirations of Airdrie in the quarter finals and Rangers in the semis. But there was a problem to be resolved regarding the jerseys.

The SFA had deemed that there was a clash of top design and demanded that the clubs should toss for the right to wear their normal strips. St Mirren won the right to play in their traditional black and white while Celtic opted for white and never wore the outfit again - it had seemingly brought them bad luck!

Up to the final Celtic, in playing five ties, had only conceded two goals. But the boys from Love Street were happy to top that stat, they had lost only one goal and that against Partick Thistle in the 3rd Round.

Right from the whistle St Mirren were firing on all

cylinders and were a goal up after only three minutes.

Davie McCrae was unceremoniously decked just outside the box and Tom Morrison's free kick was deflected for a corner. Morrison's flag kick then homed in on McCrae's cranium to nod into the net.

The irony of this early strike was that many St Mirren fans never saw the opener as they were still scrambling up the railway embankments.

Archie Findlay, Willie Newbiggin and William McDonald at the heart of the Saints defence were subjected to some severe pressure by the Celtic forwards, anxious to redeem their pride, but the Paisley men were more than equal to the task.

With just 29 minutes on the clock, St Mirren put the veneer on a cracking performance when Jimmy Howieson collected a loose ball and from all of 25 yards sent in a rocket shot which keeper Shevlin could only watch as it whistled past him.

One had to admire the courage and skill factor of the St Mirren captain and keeper big Jock Bradford, complete with his sartorially fashioned wide bunnet. He pulled off all the saves when it mattered, while up front it was Howieson and Mattha Morgan who supplied the fizz for the ever-active Davie McCrae.

The general fans view was that St Mirren were worthy winners and had done so in some style.

But, although the St Mirren fans knew they had won, there was no visible cup presentation for them.

The ceremony was conducted in what was classified as the Queen's Park Reading with the formalities being under the control of one Mr Tom White.

Now Mr White was not only the President of the SFA, he was also chairman of Celtic.

There were a few red and embarrassed faces around as his presentation speech was binned, it had been compiled to witness a Celtic win. Moral - never count your chickens!

Former St Mirren Chairman Willie Todd was only a wee boy of six when his mother and father took him to the game.

He was convinced it was parental intervention that won St Mirren that cup - his mother was attired in a brand new black and white coat!

Teams:

Celtic: *Shevlin, W. McStay, Hilley, Wilson, J. McStay, Macfarlane, Connolly, Thomson, McGrory, McInally and Leitch.*

St Mirren: *Bradford, Findlay, Newbiggin, Morrison, Summers, McDonald, Morgan, Gebbie, McCrae, Howieson and Thomson.*

Referee: *P. Craigmyle (Aberdeen).*

Attendance: *98,620.*

Willie Kelly

ST MIRREN 3 MORTON 2

SFA Summer Cup Semi Final

3rd July 1943

URING the 1939-45 years of conflict, professional soccer clubs had many a nightmare with their team selections.

Unless you were in a reserved occupation it was likely that you would be recruited to the Armed Forces. And that recruitment factor meant many players found themselves far from their football roots and resulted in team selections favouring guest players.

One can remember the redoubtable Bill Shankly, of Liverpool fame, turning out for Partick Thistle as well as Jack Howe, of Derby County, and Arthur Housam, of Sunderland, pulling on a St Mirren shirt.

However, that was small beer compared with Morton's haul of eminent players.

Can you imagine facing Stanley Matthews, Tommy Lawton and Billy Steel in the same forward line?

Matthews, the wizard of dribble, gained his first English cap when playing with Stoke City in a match against Wales in 1934 and scored on his international debut. His official cap haul was 54, his last coming against Demark in a World Cup qualifier in 1957.

No wartime games over the six year period were included and who would bet on him not achieving a 'ton up' had they all counted?

Lawton's international CV is no less impressive.

He also scored on his debut against Wales in 1938, but all his wartime caps were nullified and he went on to complete 23 England outings scoring 22 goals in the process.

With these two international heavyweights facing you, intertwined with the impressive skills of Steel, a former teenager with St Mirren, one can anticipate a feeling of anxious trepidation as Saints faced up to the Greenock side in the semi-final of this Summer Cup at Ibrox Stadium on 26th June.

If further accolades were required for this trio of stars, look no further than the Great Britain v Rest of Europe match at Hampden Park on 10th May 1947, all three contributing to the GB team winning 6-1.

A crowd of 20,000 turned up at Ibrox to take in the semi, with St Mirren holding their own and coming away with a credible 3-3 draw.

On, therefore, to Hampden Park for the replay.

In the early stages Matthews was well shadowed by young Dick McLatchie, while Willie Kelly and James Colquhoun kept Lawton on a tight rein with it all resulting in a cramped style of play.

St Mirren were slow starters and went behind after only seven minutes.

Lawton fired in a rasper, Jack Weare was well in line to make the save, but the ball ricocheted off Dick McLatchie's leg and trickled over the line. However, Lawton was given the credit for the strike.

Morton almost made it two just minutes later when a 35-yard Fyfe free kick took a sliver of paint off the crossbar.

One down at the break St Mirren had appeared somewhat lethargic, but the half time tones of encouragement from Willie Fotheringham seemed to re-energise the team.

Alex Linwood had a scoring header well saved by McPheat, but was more successful in the 52nd minute firing in the equaliser from six yards.

However, that effort only preceded another effort from Morton as Steel adroitly placed the ball in the empty net, as Weare lay injured. The big keeper had fallen heavily on his shoulder, he appeared fit to resume but after a couple of minutes he had to admit to failure - opting to continue as a limping makeshift right-winger.

Skipper Willie Kelly took over in goal with Arthur Housam donning the centre half mantle and Jimmy Stenhouse operating in the right half berth.

The re-arrangement didn't seem to upset the Saints and with 68 minutes gone Jimmy Drinkwater launched a free kick. It was destined for the Linwood cranium and a deft flick sent the ball spinning past keeper McPheat.

All Morton hopes of skill, speed and quality seemed to hit the back burner with their modus operandi now being of Route One proportions in the hope that Lawton might provide some magic.

Regretfully, all the centre forward's attempts were high, wide and generally not very handsome.

Then, just 13 minutes from the final whistle, came the winning strike. Although, in all honesty, it came as a surprise and the word fluke might have been deemed appropriate.

The ball was turned across the Morton goal by Johnny Deakin. It evaded everybody including the keeper to nestle sweetly in the corner of the net. But, there was some conjecture as to who was being credited with the goal.

Some said it was Dan McGarry's goal, but popular opinion consigned it to Deakin's memorabilia records.

However, Morton weren't finished and it took a Herculean save from makeshift keeper Kelly to keep out the lads from the Tail of the Bank.

Saints had won against all the pre-match odds and would take on Rangers in the final the following Saturday at Hampden.

Teams:

St Mirren: *Weare, Drinkwater, McLatchie, Housam, Kelly, Colquhoun, Jess, Stenhouse, Linwood, Deakin and McGarry.*

Morton: *McPheat, Maley, Fyfe, Aird McDowall, Campbell, Matthews, Garth, Lawton, Steel and Adams.*

Referee: *Mr W. Webb, Glasgow.*

Attendance: *40,000 .*

Alex Linwood

ST MIRREN 1 RANGERS 0

SFA Summer Cup Final

10th July 1943

 O appreciate this match one has to realise that wartime conditions precluded the running of the nationwide Scottish Cup and, as a morale booster for the football-starved population, a utility cup tournament was launched by the SFA.

And, in 1943, it was known as The Summer Cup.

A two-legged first round tie on the 29th May and 5th June produced a 9-4 aggregate which was enough to see off Third Lanark.

Onto the second round and an overall 7-4 return against Dumbarton ensured a well-earned semi-final placement for Saints.

As the semis were to be played at neutral venues it was deemed appropriate that both ties would be one off games with St Mirren facing our Renfrewshire neighbours Morton at Ibrox.

It always generates enormous delight to put one over on

the Cappielow side, but this pleasure had to be postponed until the following Saturday following a 3-3 draw.

This match - transferred to Hampden Park - finished in a 3-2 win for St Mirren and to savour the full flavour of that game check out the chapter dated 3rd July 1943.

On the morning of the final at Hampden Park the war-time news heralded the invasion of Sicily. Allied Forces, under the command of General Dwight D. Eisenhower, had begun landing operations early on July 10th.

However, on a much more parochial front, the SFA announced they were pegging the 1943-44 League admission prices at 1/6 for adults and 7d for boys, plus members of the Forces in uniform.

Only boys? We are pretty certain a considerable number of the fairer sex would also qualify in allocating the seven pence from their pocket money.

As for this Summer Cup Final, the stand was rated at 6/- with 4/6 being the financial output for the terracings.

A look at the Hampden playing surface confirmed a pristine pitch, but the terracings were not so well kept. They were infested with weeds, a sign of the times in procuring wartime labour to combat the unwelcome growth.

What followed brought the best out of Saints and the press had a field day proclaiming that seldom had a team with such a moderate record for the season finished the campaign with such a brilliant finale.

The St Mirren grit, skill and speed outshone their more illustrious opponents from Ibrox.

Dick McLatchie, a burgeoning teenage left back who had been signed from Hibernian only some four months earlier, hadn't really had time to express himself. His youthfulness was put to the test in combating the wiles of the Rangers' galloping winger Willie Waddell.

It was rumoured that Waddell had to have an enlarged gusset in his shorts to accommodate his lengthy stride pattern and his pace was causing alarm in the St Mirren rearguard.

Skipper Willie Kelly was on hand to provide a Polyfilla role for McLatchie filling the holes and plugging any defensive gaps.

Big George Young was fulfilling a similar role for the Ibrox side although in truth Alex Linwood's persistence was giving the Rangers stopper some trouble with some of his tackling prowess deemed to be a mite illegal according to the travelling Saints fans.

St Mirren were racking up the corner count, a useful stat because if the final wasn't decided on goals then corners would count in determining the winner. After the first 15 minutes St Mirren had logged in four flag kicks.

Paisley's finest nearly took the lead shortly prior to the interval.

Jimmy Stenhouse was a lively support to Linwood and took it on himself to thump in a 25-yarder, which crashed off Jerry Dawson's upright.

Nil-nil at the break, but popular press opinion rated St Mirren to be the better of two good sides.

The match progressed and the pace quickened with the trainers of both sides called on to administer treatment to Johnny Deakin, Kelly and keeper Dawson.

Consternation on the hour mark. Surprise, surprise, Rangers were awarded a penalty! Keeper Jack Weare had come charging out of his goal area to confront the onrushing Torry Gillick. He certainly got his hands to the ball, but Mr Godfrey decided the keeper had caught the legs of the Ibrox centre.

A soft penalty and perhaps justice prevailed when big 'Corky' Young, entrusted with the spot kick, blazed it miles wide.

Rangers upped the pressure with Saints responding where McLatchie and Jimmy Drinkwater had snuffed out any real danger from the Ibrox wingmen. When you opt for all out attack, untenanted acres appear at the back just ripe to be plundered.

It happened to Rangers in the 70th minute. Arthur Housam carried the ball well into the vacated Ibrox territory. His powerful cross was diverted by Deakin into the path of the onrushing Linwood who hooked a beauty into the corner of the net.

Cue bedlam! Linwood was engulfed by his ecstatic teammates forming a human pyramid on top of him.

Dougie Gray, the Rangers right back who became a bit of an icon at Ibrox famed for clearing numerous goal scoring chances off the Ibrox goal line, paid tribute to the scorer saying it was the finest goal he had ever seen at Hampden.

Time slowly passed minute by minute for the Saints fans.

They had cottoned onto the fact that history was possibly here in the making.

But, their backs were to the proverbial wall. Indeed, if corners had to count to settle the tie, then Rangers would have needed an abacus to tally up their flag-kick collection.

Three minutes from time Rangers should have equalised when Jimmy Duncanson, later to join St Mirren, was clean through on goal.

Parity was in sight for Rangers but keeper Jack Weare, on leave from the RAF, flung himself at Duncanson's feet to make a cup winning save of outstanding quality sending the ginger haired inside man into virtual orbit.

St Mirren were worthy winners with Douglas Bowie, President of the SFA, making the presentations with each player receiving National Savings Certificates with seven going to each of the winners and three to the runners up.

Back to Paisley for the celebrations with the trophy being taken to the Victory Theatre Variety Show where both evening performances were interrupted as the team and the Summer Cup took a well-earned bow.

Teams:

St Mirren: *Weare, Drinkwater, McLatchie, Housam, Kelly, Colquhoun, Jess, Stenhouse, Linwood, Deakin and McGarry.*

Rangers: *Dawson, Gray, Shaw, Little, Young, Symon, Waddell, Duncanson, Gillick, Venters and Johnstone.*

Referee: *Mr J.S. Godfrey, Stenhousemuir.*

Attendance: *46,000.*

Jimmy Drinkwater

KILMARNOCK 1 ST MIRREN 5

League Division A

5th April 1947

 VER the years Morton have been clearly designated as St Mirren's local derby opposition.

But when the Cappielow club found themselves occasionally slipping down the relegation ladder to the lower league depths it was Kilmarnock who supplied the need as St Mirren's derby day opponents.

As a result many a ding-dong materialised and this April encounter would be no different as both clubs were within a touch in facing relegation, the other contenders being Hamilton and Queen's Park.

Without a scheduled fixture on the last day of March, manager Bobby Rankin was keen to keep his players fully tuned for the Rugby Park game and arranged a friendly with Division B side Ayr United at their Somerset Park home.

More than 4,000 fans took in this bounce game with the Honest Men - the match ending in a 1-1 draw with the diminutive Arthur Milne netting Saints' goal.

One major pre-match worry for Rankin was the fitness of left back Davie Lindsay.

He had taken a bad knee injury in Saints last league outing against Third Lanark at Love Street and the loss of the doughty defender would be a tremendous loss to the Buddies' defensive set up.

Lindsay had generated a widespread reputation in the Scottish game as a tough tackling full back with many a right winger breathing a sigh of relief at the news if Lindsay wasn't listed in the St Mirren line up.

Lindsay was also in the news transfer wise. David Jack, the Middlesbrough manager, had money to spend. And he had his eye on a clutch of players north of the border having already lured the St Mirren icon Alex Linwood to Ayresome Park.

The Jack shopping list included Billy Steel, of Morton, Motherwell's Jimmy Watson as well as Lindsay. Needless to say his sweet talking overtures were firmly rebuffed at Love Street.

One other pre match worry for the Saints management team was the likely state of the Rugby Park pitch. Days prior to the game saw the mercury plummet to -10 degrees Celsius with the prospect of icy conditions to contend with.

As happens with the changeable Scottish weather, it wasn't frost that greeted the travelling Saints team, it was a day of hurricane winds and monsoon conditions.

Lindsay didn't make the starting eleven with Sam Smith taking his place and Malcolm McLaren replacing Archie Aikman from the Ayr United game.

What a day for St Mirren!

Kilmarnock were outplayed and out-manoeuvred by a fast-thinking, fast-moving Paisley outfit and now facing a very real relegation threat.

In conditions that produced some weird and wonderful moments, the outstanding classic feature of the game was a hat trick by Jimmy Drinkwater - and what a collector's item his threesome turned out to be.

After Killie's John Devlin had handled in the box, Drinkwater twice saw the gale force wind blow the ball off the penalty spot. It was finally secured in position thanks to the collective efforts of referee Davidson and a couple of 'Drinkie's' team mates.

Keeper Mitchell Downie, who had the unnerving job of waiting while this scenario was being enacted, did manage to get his hands to the penalty strike but the pace beat him.

Then a real hat-trick treat.

Trailing 2-1 at the break, Kilmarnock kicked off in the second half with the ball being swung over to the left flank. Drinkwater managed to intercept it in his own half, tried an up and under and then saw the ball soar down wind before bouncing over the head of advancing keeper Downie for a goal in a million!

Pantomime stuff really, but this was a relegation match with Saints happy to go 3-1 up.

The third Drinkwater strike was a free kick just outside the box, the ball being wind assisted and ricocheting off the Kilmarnock wall.

McLaren and Johnny Deakin were the other contributors to the St Mirren goal haul while Devlin notched Kilmarnock's sole crumb of comfort with a 35 yard free kick with the wind causing the ball to swerve in flight, completely wrong footing Malcolm Newlands in the St Mirren goal.

St Mirren's lightweight attack was always dangerous and ready to deploy a shoot-on-sight policy, whereas the Killie boys were over elaborate in their build up.

Hood, Turnbull and McAvoy offered most for the home side with Newlands, Willie Telfer, Alex Crowe, Drinkwater and Deakin being outstanding Buddies.

Postscript: Kilmarnock failed to beat the drop with Hamilton Accies joining them in Division B.

Teams:

Kilmarnock: *Downie, Hood, Landsborough, Turnbull, Thyne, Devlin, Stevenson, Reid, Collins, McAvoy and Drury.*

St Mirren: *Newlands, Telfer, Smith, Drinkwater, Roy, Cunningham, Stenhouse, Crowe, Milne, McLaren and Deakin.*

Referee: *W. Davidson (Glasgow).*

Estimated Attendance: *8,000.*

Bobby Rankin

ST MIRREN 7 QUEEN OF THE SOUTH 1

League Cup Competition

6th September 1947

THE advent of the Second World War saw hostilities with Germany plunge Scottish football into total confusion.

Only five games in a 20-team Division One were played before the Scottish League authorities pulled the plug.

The Government didn't want massed groups of football spectators to congregate at set times thus offering the prospects of carnage and chaos to the rampaging German Luftwaffe.

As a compromise, as far as St Mirren's competitive terrain was concerned, the Scottish League became the Southern League with membership being restricted to teams from the central belt.

In effect St Mirren competed in a 16-team league.

Equally, the Scottish Cup went to the wall being replaced

by the Southern League Cup, again with 16 competing teams operating in four sectionalised groups. In the first war- time year of competition in 1941, St Mirren reached the semi final stage losing out 4-1 to Rangers at Hampden Park.

With the end of the war, that Southern League Cup assumed its national identity as the Scottish League Cup with 31 teams in competition in season 1946-47.

In the second year of national competition in 1947-48 St Mirren found their section soulmates to be Aberdeen, Motherwell and Queen of the South.

Pre-season speculation as to the section winners seemed to have the bookmaking fraternity favouring Aberdeen.

Motherwell were also considered a force with the later St Mirren manager Wilson Humphries leading the Fir Park charge.

As for Saints, Aberdeen and Motherwell would be tough games, but The Doonhamers from Dumfries shouldn't pose a problem.

That was the considered opinion until Saturday 16th August with an away day to Palmerston Park on the cards.

The bookmaking boys offered favourable odds for the Fertile Four, these being the games between Aberdeen and Motherwell, Celtic and Dundee, Hibernian and Clyde and, of course, Queen of the South and St Mirren. Never has a bet been so favourably titled, Queens were more than fertile they were abundantly prolific!

To say that Saints were humiliated would be a gross understatement.

An 8-1 defeat in any language is a veritable drubbing. Among the Dumfries marksmen was the future Scotland centre Billy Houliston who netted two. St Mirren's sole counter came from Johnny Deakin.

But Johnny wasn't a happy laddie. The Wednesday before the return game with Queens, Deakin received a letter from manager Bobby Rankin advising him his request for a transfer had been turned down.

After 10 years at Love Street, Deakin felt he needed a

change of environment, allied of course to an increase in his pay packet. It might have been the thought that there was a mood of discordance in the Love Street ranks, but no it was Bobby Rankin who masterminded some recruitment with his limited resources.

With match admission prices not being particularly conducive to large transfer fees, after all a stand seat would cost you 3/- in old money with 1/6 giving you access to the terracing and if you were a laddie your pocket money required 7d for entry, unless you were fly enough to get an illegal lift over the turnstile.

The wizardly skills of Rankin produced one Gerry Burrell, brought over from the Dundela club in Belfast and later to assume the nickname of the Belfast Buddie. Allied to Burrell's arrival was a Polish serviceman Alfons Lesz.

But, the Saints faithful couldn't get their tongues around the Alfons bit and were more than happy with a Paisley Alfie!

Three weeks since the Dumfries debacle this return match at the Love Street Grounds, as the press were wont to call St Mirren's home patch, provided the anticipated headlines of a 'Revenge Match.'

St Mirren would have to go some way to erase the memory of that 8-1 scoreline.

It didn't take Saints long to open the revenge match account. Willie Jack had a point blank drive saved by keeper Wilson in the first minute, but it took the centre only another couple of minutes to open the scoring by heading home a neat lob from Jimmy Drinkwater.

Jimmy Stenhouse, a sturdy little character, scored the second in using his considerable physique to muscle his way past two Queens defenders to neatly loft the ball over the Palmerston keeper.

Saints were two up and cruising thanks to the Queen of the South half back line, who were being over run and seemed all at sea - mal de mere at its worst.

Wee Alfie Lesz whacked in number three in the 20th minute and eight minutes later his name was on the scorecard again when he headed powerfully past Wilson.

Four up at the break, manager Rankin's half time words of wisdom were simple - 'Go out and enjoy yourselves.'

There was a different scenario in the Dumfries dressing room.

The resultant verbal tirade certainly seemed to energise Queens, although their game plan seemed to revolve around the limitation of a dubious offside trap.

The tactics didn't worry Messrs Jack and Burrell who helped themselves to numbers five and six. Late in the game a scoring header from Jack gave Saints front man his hat trick.

Just before the final whistle Jenkins knocked in a consolation goal for the Doonhamers.

The post match advice for the St Mirren lads was simply not to gloat over this performance.

It was totally adequate, but was helped in no small way by an under strength and exceedingly poor Queen of the South team. Still, the mauling in Dumfries had been avenged.

Post match stats revealed that the spring heeled Willie Jack, with eight goals in his first six games for Saints, was top of the Division 'A' scoring charts, whereas Queen of the South hadn't found the net prior to the Dumfries game with Saints and their eight goal pillage made them the second highest scoring side in the country.

Postscript: As predicted Aberdeen went on to top the section, but only heading Motherwell on goal difference.

Teams:

St Mirren: *Rennie, Drinkwater, Smith, Hunter, Telfer, Martin, Burrell, Stenhouse, Jack, Lesz and Milne.*

Queen of the South: *Wilson, Savage, James, Scott, Mundell, Sharp, Nutley, Dempsey, Baker, Jenkins and Johnstone.*

Referee: *Mr J.M. Martin, Blairgowrie.*

Estimated Attendance: *10,000*

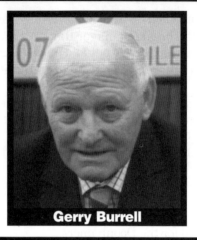

Gerry Burrell

ST MIRREN 6 MORTON 1

Renfrewshire Cup Final

24th August 1948

HERE is no doubt the Paisley folk have an extensive catalogue of mouth watering occasions and these are not necessary related to the culinary arts.

One such feel-good factor near the top of the pecking orders must surely be to witness arriving holiday baggage appearing on the carousel at nearby Glasgow Airport. The potential feeling of luggage loss vanishes at speed.

In 1948 the Paisley fraternity would be returning after their annual local holiday fortnight and on the football menu might be another heart-warming occasion - a St Mirren meeting with old Renfrewshire rivals Morton hoping to hump their County cousins in the final of the Renfrewshire Cup.

Saying goodbye to the summer season saw British Rail advertising a final Clyde coast cruise to Campbeltown rated at a 12/6 return. Down at the Oval, in London, the Australian pace men Ray Lindwall and Keith Miller were causing chaos in the final test.

Caught on a drying wicket, England were all out for 52 in their first innings with Len Hutton scoring 39 of them.

Nearer home, still on the cricket front, former St Mirren man Willie Nichol was doing his stuff for Kelburne against Kilmarnock at Whitehaugh - top scoring with 44 and taking 6 for 27.

Certainly the new football season build-up wasn't cloaked in glamorous pre-season games with the high and mighty, a much more homely and leisurely programme was assembled.

A clutch of 5-a-side tournaments centred on the salubrious surrounds of Millport and Rothesay with these warm-ups preceding the annual St Mirren trial match, where the alphabetically listed 'A' team took on the ham and eggers collectively listed as the 'B' side.

Saints came out of the league traps firing on all cylinders.

Both Johnny Deakin and Alfie Lesz picked up injuries in the trial match and missed out on the first league fixture against Clyde at Love Street. However, Li'l Arthur Milne was on hand to score twice in the 2-1 win.

On to Cliftonhill Stadium, in Coatbridge, for a midweek confrontation with Albion Rovers. Another 2-1 result for Saints and again it was the diminutive Mr Milne who racked up both goals.

Now the Renfrewshire Cup Final was on the near horizon, but before that cup get together the small matter of a league fixture had to be fulfilled against our County rivals at Love Street.

Again Saints posted a 2-1 result in their favour and, after three league games, St Mirren were top of the First Division and the only club with full points.

Regretfully, it seemed as though Morton failed to treat this cup final seriously.

The previous evening they took off to the Borders to play a match against a Southern Counties select side and scored nine.

The select team scored four and, while class goalkeeper Jimmy Cowan was in the Cappielow side's line up for the league match, he opted to play in the Southern Counties game rather than face St Mirren again at Love Street.

Although both sides were vastly under their normal league strength, St Mirren on this showing had a greater depth of reserve talent than Morton.

In fact, some of their established regulars had to look to their laurels to retain their places.

Gerry Burrell had indicated his thirst for goals in scoring both counters in the league match and went on to trump that performance by netting four.

The St Mirren attack paid out its first dividend when Burrell took on the advancing keeper and comprehensively beat him with an audacious side step.

Morton had their first real chance when McGarrity dummied keeper Willie Miller, but Mulgrew was too slow off his mark and the chance was wasted.

The ever-alert Willie Jack made it two when he intercepted a faulty pass back from a free kick from Henderson to his keeper. The Morton goalie was not a happy chappie.

After the break, Jack and company were soon back laying a siege to the Cappielow goal.

Stevenson had to move lively to save a drive from Burrell, but the Belfast Buddie, as he was known, wasn't to be denied and quickly knocked in another two goals to complete his hat trick and put the rampant Paisley side four up.

Shortly afterwards that Irish leprechaun, guising as Burrell, added his fourth and Saints fifth.

Morton managed to open their account when Jimmy Drinkwater illegally decked Cupples in the box and Campbell's spot kick sent keeper Miller the wrong way.

St Mirren were hungry for more goals and John Telford obliged with a neat header for number six.

Established in 1878-79, this was the 64th year of The Renfrewshire Cup and the respective scores to date are Morton with 24 and St Mirren just out in front with 26 wins. Close!

Teams:

St Mirren: *Miller, Smith, Drinkwater, G. Wilson, Telfer, Willie Reid, Burrell, Crowe, Jack, Davie and Telford.*

Morton: *Stevenson, Henderson, Whigham, Campbell, Miller, White, Alexander, Farquhar, Cupples, McGarrity and Mulgrew.*

Referee: *F. Scott, Paisley.*

Alex Crowe

ST MIRREN 5 HEART OF MIDLOTHIAN 5

Scottish League Cup

18th August 1951

THOSE with aspirations of achieving a millionaire lifestyle generated from success in the treble chance circuits will have no doubt extended thanks to St Mirren on many an occasion for satisfying their thirst from the catalogue of Saints' drawn games.

These have been plentiful from 0-0s, 1-1s, 2-2s and 3-3s registered in abundance, to even a 4-4 scoreline with St Mirren and Raith Rovers drawing their league match at Love Street, in April 1913.

But the drawn match that takes the biscuit is the sectionalised League Cup game with Hearts on August 18th 1951 when the two teams shared 10 goals!

St Mirren were a mite-ill prepared for this game, as keeper John Lynch was injured yet again and young Len Crabtree, a signing from Cumnock Juniors, took over between the sticks.

Also missing were Davie Lapsley, in the middle of a

contractual dispute, plus 'Togo' Johnston, George Stewart and the mercurial Alfie Lesz.

Against a Hearts side that hit the action running and racked up a first half 3-1 lead, the Paisley folk settled down to yet another drubbing being made all the more miserable by the steady downpour.

Yet there was a silver lining with the home crowd rubbing their eyes in disbelief as their favourites fought back with vim and vigour to draw level at half time.

Again, in the second half, Hearts restored their two-goal lead and once more the comeback kings that were Saints wrote the score off and indeed, could even have snatched a win at the end.

St Mirren won the toss and within a minute were a goal down.

Johnny Urquhart made tracks down the Hearts left wing, drew keeper Crabtree and laid the ball on a plate for Willie Bauld to tap in.

The Edinburgh pressure was intense and it was a bit of a surprise when St Mirren equalised. Gerry Burrell beat McSpadyen to a loose ball, headed for the bye-line and delivered a pass to Eddie Blyth who steered the ball into Alex Crowe's path and the centre duly delivered.

Willie Bauld, styled as 'The King of Hearts' by the Tynecastle fans, was outstanding with his close dribbling and it was no surprise when he netted a second.

Indeed, young Crabtree was somewhat all at sea with the bewildering speed of the Hearts forwards. It certainly wasn't to be his day and he was stretchered off suffering a head injury with Joe Martin taking over the goalkeeping duties.

Crabtree did return to the fray later, but his concussed state only gave him a fitness factor to trot up and down the right wing.

Bauld made it 3-1 for his hat trick and the entire Hearts team were rampant at this point.

But Saints weren't finished. Cox and Parker cleared net bound efforts off the line before Eddie Blyth sent over a beauty of a free kick for Crowe to score his second.

Buoyed with this score, Saints turned up the heat and when Blyth robbed Bobby Parker his cross was crashed home by Gerry Burrell for the equaliser. Three each at the break.

McSpadyen was another to be stretchered off, but managed to return to provide a limited contribution on the Hearts right wing. That contribution extended to a lame duck cross with Bauld being the grateful recipient. Number four for both Hearts and Bauld.

Hearts went further ahead in controversial circumstances. Jimmy Wardhaugh raced through the Saints defence and, with only Martin to beat, slipped the ball to Bauld who netted easily. Willie Telfer and the St Mirren defence were furious claiming the goal to be offside. Referee Jack Mowat was having none of it and booked Telfer for his OTT outburst.

Led by the wiles of the diminutive Blyth, St Mirren launched attack after attack. Indeed, Jimmy Brown in the Hearts goal brought off the save of the match to thwart Crowe. But Alex wasn't to be denied and scored to make it 5-4 to Hearts.

With only seven minutes left Blyth again supplied some left wing magic and sent over another quality cross for Crowe to head home his fourth and the Saints equaliser. Cue bedlam on the Paisley terraces.

Could St Mirren snatch a winner? Almost, but not quite. It was Burrell who raced clear of the opposition only to be downed in the box. Everyone with a Paisley affinity screamed PENALTY, but referee Mowat said no and was immediately crossed off the Paisley Christmas card lists.

To score five goals in a match, while outstanding, was not a surprise from a player as goal hungry as Bauld.

In logging in 510 appearances for the Tynecastle club, he netted a remarkable 355 goals thanks in many ways to his inside forward cohorts of Alfie Conn and Jimmy Wardhaugh.

Crowe wasn't quite so prolific in the goal grabbing stakes

thanks in no small way to two broken legs. However, he did start in 93 games over a six-season period and netted a scoring return of 33. Clearly that quartet against Hearts was the jewel in his goal-scoring crown.

Teams:

St Mirren: *Crabtree, Drinkwater, Ashe, Neilson, Telfer, Martin, Burrell, Rice, Crowe, Goldthorpe and Blyth.*

Hearts: *Brown, Parker, McSpadyen, Whithead, Dougan, Cox, Sloan, Wardhaugh, Bauld, Cumming and Urquhart.*

Referee: *Jack Mowat MBE, Rutherglen.*

Attendance: 12,000.

Jackie Neilson

QUEEN OF THE SOUTH 2   ST MIRREN 7

League Division A

11th September 1954

IT was the usual custom in the 1950s to start the playing season with the League Cup campaign.

The 32 clubs were sectioned into eight mini leagues with St Mirren's bedfellows being Motherwell, Kilmarnock and Raith Rovers.

Saints failed to top their section and thus lost out on a quarter final placement. However, they were the top scorers in their group with 15 goals, but regretfully they also topped the goals conceded total with 14.

Big John McGrory was the leading net finder with six goals including a cracking hat trick against Motherwell at Love Street.

The Fir Park side went on to reach the final, losing out in a 4-2 scoreline to Hearts.

The Love Street brigade were therefore seemingly in reasonable good heart for this opening round of league fixtures which sent them down to Dumfries to take on the residents of Palmerston Park.

Saints hadn't beaten Queen of the South on their own patch since pre-war days - September 1936 to be precise- so, would season 54-55 be a turning point?

For the opening game Bobby Holmes and Jimmy Mallan came in to the team from the last League Cup line-up.

The result tells the whole story - Queen of the South were no match for a classic St Mirren performance.

Yet the match provided a lesson for Saints - an object lesson in complacency.

Chances were missed whereas in other tense games the lacklustre occasions could have caused serious damage to the final result.

Despite this criticism the Buddies were happy to play a brand of football that completely mesmerised the 'Doonhamers.'

However, being super-critical, Willie Telfer and Jackie Neilson were not up to their usual high standard, yet the collective output of the entire defence was way above normal.

The return of Holmes from injury was a classic move.

Apart from providing a solid look in his wing-half domain, Holmes' arsenal of pinpoint passes were eagerly digested by Tommy Gemmell.

In turn, the wee man from Mossblown was at his imperial best and brought top form out of Gordon McMaster, David Laird, John McGrory and Brian Callan who all played out of their skins.

Compared to Queens, the Saints were faster to the ball, were faster on it and found their men with a series of classic interchanges.

McMaster had his best game to date out on the wing while Laird, until his injury, was only a shade behind Gemmell. Never-say-die Callan played not only with his feet but also with his head.

Big McGrory netted a couple and, bar for some goalkeeping heroics from Roy Henderson, the bustling centre might have had a hat trick.

This was the era when Glasgow had four main line railway stations, with St Enoch's being the departure point for Dumfries. However, the train was a quarter of an hour late in leaving St Enoch's and 25 minutes late in arriving at Dumfries. To save time the St Mirren players went into the guard's van and changed into pants, boots and stockings.

Callan had an unfortunate altercation with an Ayrshire vandal. Just outside Sanquhar station a missile shattered the glass in the corridor and Callan was struck on the back of his neck with a glass shard.

Willie Telfer won the toss and within the first three minutes St Mirren had forced four corners - the Saints meant business.

They opened the scoring in the 14th minute with the diminutive Gemmell getting on the end of a knock-down by McGrory to send the ball over Henderson's flailing arms.

On the half hour a mistake by Henderson allowed Laird to set McMaster free to edge the ball over the line. Eight minutes from the tea break the game was done and dusted when a classic cross from McMaster was powerfully headed home by McGrory.

Gemmell made it four with one of his specials. He jinked, twisted and turned his way through the entire Queens' defence and proceeded to bamboozle the keeper by sending him the wrong way.

Queens came out for the second half having been subjected to a blistering tirade from their manager. Their new found resolve saw a number of attacks launched, but it was St Mirren who found the net for number five when Laird's blistering speed outpaced his marker and sent a pass to McMaster allowing the winger to drive home under Henderson's diving body.

With many of the Doonhamer fans now deserting the terracings they failed to see outside right Black reduce the leeway with a first class drive past Lornie.

St Mirren were far from finished and in the 77th minute Gemmell made the opening for McGrory to fire in Saints' sixth with a drive off the upright.

In a late foray into the St Mirren defensive zone, McGill was unceremoniously decked in the box with Binning converting the spot kick. Two minutes from time Callan made it seven up.

Teams:

Queen of the South: *Henderson, Sharp, Binning, Campbell, Smith, Greenock, Black, McGill, Brown, Adams and Oakes.*

St Mirren: *Lornie, Lapsley, Mallan, Neilson, Telfer, Holmes, McMaster, Laird, McGrory, Gemmell and Callan.*

Referee: *Hugh Phillips (Wishaw).*

Estimated Attendance: *9,000.*

Willie Telfer

ABERDEEN 2 ST MIRREN 1

Scottish League Cup Final

22nd October 1955

THE Spoilers starring Rory Calhoun, Anne Baxter and Jeff Chandler was the current film on show at the Paisley cinema outlets.

It was also on show at Hampden Park in what was St Mirren's first ever taste of the League Cup final proceedings.

The weans were greetin' that a big bad boy had pinched all their sweeties. That was the Paisley speak. In a translation for the 'greetin' weans' read the travelling St Mirren fan base, for the 'big bad boy' step forward Aberdeen Football Club, as for the 'sweeties' it was the League Cup that was effectively stolen. This was grand larceny big time!

The media headlines said it all. *'Dithering Aberdeen got most of the breaks in a Hampden thriller'*

'A fluke floors Saints'

'The Dons on a trophy steal'

The breaks certainly deserted St Mirren.

Brian Callan on the Saints left wing - and the strong man of the Love Street forward line - picked up an early injury in the first half and had to swap wings with Jim Rodger.

The early television news bulletins were highlighting that the pre-Christmas hype was already in full flight for the retail stores - and it was still only mid-October!

Aberdeen went one better - they brought Santa Claus to Hampden and went home with a gift-wrapped trophy.

It was a fairly even fought first half.

The press had clearly marked the Buddies card as cup final runners-up and the resultant chip on their black and white garbed shoulders was understandable as they took the field with all guns blazing.

Wee Tommy Gemmell chased everything in that first quarter of an hour. With such a miniscule frame as his, it begs the question, 'Just where does he buy his energy from - his tank is always full?'

After the initial bursts of speed from the Granite City wing men, Graham Leggat and Jackie Hather were confined to savour only crumbs of soccer comfort and started to roam in search of some meaningful football sustenance.

Willie Telfer had Paddy Buckley secured in his back pocket which left a monumental task for the Dons inside men and Yorston and Wishart couldn't handle it.

The Dons needed a break and after a no scoring first period they luckily got the opener in the 47th minute.

The Pittodrie outside left Jackie Hather whipped over a fierce cross into the Saints goalmouth. Keeper Jim Lornie and Leggat were both beaten by the pace of the ball. Jimmy Mallan came in to defend his goal, couldn't get out of the way, the ball hit his back and then trickled over the line for a freakish goal.

Jim Clunie, later to feature with St Mirren both as a player and the manager, was providing some sterling stuff in keeping the tabs on Brown, the livewire Saints centre, and even had time to help curtail the Paisley wingmen.

Saints upped the pressure with the Dons forced to concede a clutch of free kicks all from a mouth-watering position just outside the penalty area. The strong going Jackie Neilson neatly piloted one of these kicks into the box for Bobby Holmes to direct a diving header past Fred Martin.

The Paisley tails were up but then another tragedy came their way. David Laird collapsed after a less than friendly tackle. He received some trainer attention but was only able to offer a half-cocked contribution to the fray.

If these set backs weren't enough, worse was to follow in the 79th minute.

Way out on the right flank the flier that was Leggat was being shepherded wide by a couple of the Saints defenders. He was only a yard or two from the touchline when he managed to launch a speculative left foot cross towards the St Mirren goalmouth.

Jim Lornie never expected a shot from that distance. The ball sailed and swerved in the Hampden swirl; it deceived Lornie, floated over his head and slithered down the inside of the net.

An excited Dons fan labelled it as a goal in a million. Those of a Paisley persuasion would call it a downright fluke. Any neutrals in the crowd would probably tag it a bit of both.

So, 2-1 to the Granite City team and after the final whistle Aberdeen manager Davie Shaw, the former Hibernian and Scotland left back, came into the Saints dressing room. His words were spiced with reality.

He said: 'Hard luck boys. I know just how you are feeling. I've often been in that position myself.

'And, while I must be happy that my club has won the cup, I tell you in all sincerity that I think we were dammed lucky.'

Every Paisley patron endorsed his thoughts.

Teams:
Aberdeen: *Martin, Mitchell, Caldwell, Wilson, Clunie, Glen, Leggat, Yorston, Buckley, Wishart and Hather.*
St Mirren: *Lornie, Lapsley, Mallan, Neilson, Telfer, Holmes, Rodger, Laird, Brown, Gemmell and Callan.*
Referee: *Hugh Phillips, Motherwell.*
Attendance: *44,106.*

Bobby Holmes

PARTICK THISTLE 1   ST MIRREN 5

Scottish Cup 5th Round 2nd Replay

11th February 1957

THE format of the 1956-57 Scottish Cup tourney brought together a galaxy of non-league clubs, Highland League sides as well as teams from the East and South of Scotland Leagues.

With no disrespect in any way, many of these clubs had to be weeded out prior to the entry of the more established league teams.

The 1st Round started way back in September and it was February before St Mirren were introduced to the 5th Round with a home tie to take on the might of Partick Thistle.

The first tie ended in a 1-1 draw with the replay at Firhill being equally indecisive and a 2-2 result the final outcome.

It has been known in selecting a venue for a second replay to be determined by a toss of a coin, but on this occasion the SFA management decided the third meeting would take place at Hampden Park.

If a Man of the Match covering all three games had to be nominated it would have to be the redoubtable Bobby Holmes.

As in the first two games Partick Thistle were first to score and in the Love Street and Firhill encounters Holmes, a wing half operating as an inside forward, came to the Buddies rescue.

Holmes netted the equaliser in the first tie and scored both goals in the second. And in the Hampden Park decider he rose to head the goal that forced the game to extra time.

After this marathon tie of 330 minutes, it was St Mirren who ended Partick Thistle's interest in the cup and so qualified to meet Dunfermline in the 6th Round at Love Street.

The Buddies deserved their extra time win, albeit it was achieved against opposition forced through injury to field five reserve players.

At the outset St Mirren collared the initiative with Partick Thistle labouring as a collection of units rather than an organised whole.

In the first half hour the Firhill fellows might have been at least two goals down. They escaped that punishment due to the slothfulness of the Love Street attack, plus a catalogue of outstanding saves from keeper Tommy Ledgerwood.

Yet the biggest miss in the first half came at the other end when Matt Crowe, in total isolation in front of the Saints goal, only had to pick his spot when he managed to blaze the offering high over the Buddies bar.

The inside man made amends within less than a minute after the restart when he squared to the unmarked Davie McParland who drove home an angled shot past the oncoming Saints keeper Campbell Forsyth.

For some 15 minutes or so Partick Thistle's confidence factor rose and they played at last like a cohesive unit. There was now a jauntiness about the Jags with a mirrored anxiety now appearing on the Paisley foreheads.

On the 78th minute mark Holmes restored some Love Street confidence when he steered his cranium to make contact with a Willie Devine free kick to head the equaliser past Ledgerwood.

St Mirren upped the pace and went all out for the winner but they were lacking in a modicum of guile to unhinge the 'Maryhill Magyars.'

And so to extra time with Willie Telfer wearing his centre forward hat and racing in on the Thistle goal when Andy Kerr unfairly decked the striker just outside the 18-yard line.

This was Davie Lapsley country with the Saints full back thundering in a classic Lapsley strike that took a marginal deflection giving Ledgerwood no chance.

Just 11 minutes later Devine sent over a peach of a cross that Telfer nodded down for Willie McCulloch to lash into the roof of the net from an almost impossible angle.

Partick Thistle were now down and out and when Davie Lapsley launched an up and under into the Firhill goalmouth it was a seemingly easy take for keeper Ledgerwood but he fumbled, dropped the ball and McCulloch walked the ball over the line.

But the Saints scoring tally wasn't finished yet. Devine was on a charge on goal only to have his nose illegally introduced to the Hampden turf by full back Bobby Gibb a mere yard just outside the box.

The Partick Thistle defence stood awaiting another Lapsley thunderbolt, but Telfer cheekily, and unexpectedly, drove it home to make it 5-1 in Saints favour.

The three ties attracted an overall aggregate of 51,736 with the Hampden game takings realising £1,291 - a nice little earner for both clubs.

Postscript: St Mirren went on to defeat Dunfermline 1-0 in the 7th Round, but lost out 2-1 to Celtic in the quarter finals.

Teams:

Partick Thistle: *Ledgerwood, Kerr, Gibb, Thomson, McNab, Mathers, McKenzie, McParland, Smith, Crowe and Ewing.*

St Mirren: *Forsyth, Lapsley, J. Wilson, S. Wilson, Dallas, Johnstone, Devine, Gemmell, Telfer, Holmes and McCulloch.*

Referee: *R.H. Davidson.*

Attendance: *13,387.*

Tommy Bryceland

HIBERNIAN 5 ST MIRREN 5

League Division One

22nd February 1958

PAISLEY natives and in particular those with a St Mirren persuasion, were a mite nervous and on the warpath.

The 1957-58 Scottish Cup campaign had seen Saints see off Ayr United in the first round and then only after a replay at home.

Next up in Round 2 saw Dunfermline visiting Love Street.

The Pars were in Division Two. Should be a coupon home win certainty, but in effect it became a veritable coupon buster.

The 4-1 defeat did little to appease the faithful.

For most of the game the Love Street Saints had given the impression of being locked in a funereal warp.

Indeed, they all sported black armbands, but that plus a one minute silence, was in sympathy for all the Manchester United players who had perished in the Munich air disaster.

Much of the disquiet had emanated from the transfer of Willie Telfer to Rangers back in November and now, out of the cup and flirting with relegation, the fans began to rattle the St Mirren cage.

A concerted number of bullet points were proffered and voiced, with five of the best being:

1. Foster a more up market spirit by getting to the root of the current dispirited efforts.

2. Dispense with the services of the manager if he is only to be an office boy and a figurehead - someone to whom the buck can be passed.

3. Appoint a qualified coach.

4. Give him the players to work with so that they think football night and day.

5. Appoint two working directors - young men of some knowledge and ability and give them their full say at all board meetings.

Clearly the high degree of vitriolic outpourings would in no way be assuaged overnight with manager Willie Reid taking the brunt of their displeasure.

Morale was seemingly at an almighty low for the next game away to Hibernian at Easter Road.

It was the euphoric Jimmy Greaves, he of 57 England caps and a ready quip as a media pundit in later years, who coined the nugget - 'Football's a funny old game.'

The match at Easter Road was more than funny - it was more than comical. In fact, it went some way to appeasing the dispirited Saints support.

The newspaper headlines said it all. 'Stupendous! Colossal! Amazing! Incredible!'

This 5-5 draw was one of St Mirren's finest hours with both managers - Reid of St Mirren and Hugh Shaw at Easter Road - in a quandary as to whether to berate their defences for shipping five goals or congratulating their strikers for a quintet of the best.

The man primarily responsible in orchestrating the turnaround for St Mirren was left half Jimmy Thomson. Stationed with the Army at Aldershot, Thomson was a half back par excellence with bite in the tackle, a wide range of sweeping passes, combined with the intelligent use of the open space.

St Mirren skipper Jackie Neilson said post-game re-Thomson, 'The boy played a great game.'

Such a mouthing from the hard-to-please captain was an accolade in itself.

John 'Cockles' Wilson kicked off with Saints taking the lead after just two minutes. Wee Tommy Gemmell took a pass from Wilson and proceeded to waltz round keeper Leslie to steer the ball over the line.

However, just two minutes later Hibs were level.

Full back John Higgins brought of a full-length goalkeeping save to deny Joe Baker.

In the current climate Mr Higgins would have seen red, however in 1958 he escaped such punishment with Eddie Turnbull enjoying belting home the penalty equaliser.

Still the goals kept coming with Thomson and Gemmell combining to set up Tommy Bryceland for Saints second.

The unbelievable was happening with St Mirren exorcising their football cobwebs by going further ahead midway through the half with Bryceland clipping the ball well out of Leslie's reach.

St Mirren were 3-1 up, but they took the foot off the gas pedal and allowed Willie Ormond and Baker to restore parity at the tea break.

Only two minutes after the interval St Mirren took the lead again. Bryceland sent a lob into the box and Vincent Ryan, a signing from Celtic and making his black and white debut, headed home for his first St Mirren goal.

Hibs drew level once more when their member of clan Thomson met a cross from Ormond to head past the helpless keeper Jim Lornie.

Hibs were now on the rampage and Higgins again repeated his goalkeeping party piece by stopping an Ormond drive with his hands. Turnbull took the spot-kick, only for Lornie to parry his effort. But Turnbull followed up to give Hibs the lead for the first time in the match.

Then 11 minutes from time newcomer Ryan scampered up the wing and from his cross Wilson nudged the ball home. Final score 5-5!

Last week sinners! This week gold plated Saints! You'd better believe it.

Teams:

Hibernian: *Leslie, MacFarlane, McClelland, Turnbull, Paterson, Baxter, Fraser, Thomson, Baker, Preston and Ormond.*

St Mirren: *Lornie, Lapsley, Higgins, Neilson, Buchanan, Thomson, Bryceland, Ryan, Wilson, Gemmell and Johnston.*

Referee: *P. Fitzpatrick.*

Estimated Attendance: *10,000.*

Joe & Gerry Baker

ST MIRREN 2 HIBERNIAN 1

League Division One

22nd November 1958

THIS was the football era when the first team played at home while the Reserve side played away on the same day.

So, in welcoming Hibernian to Love Street, the St Mirren Reserves were on duty over at Easter Road.

Ironically, Cecil B. Demille's film production of 'The Ten Commandments' was showing at the late, lamented Kelburne Cinema with admission to the 'flicks' costing 3/6, 5/6 and 7/6.

The intrigue in Paisley was that the Reserves were lampooned in Edinburgh to the tune of 10-2! Did the worthy Mr Demille know something that we didn't?

The pre-match game plan saw Ian Riddell about to play watchdog over the Scotland and Hibernian outside right Gordon Smith - not everyone's idea of a stress-free afternoon.

Riddell was making his first team debut as both John

'Cockles' Wilson and John McTurk were sidelined through injury.

The Hibs man was affectionately termed the 'Gay Gordon', not a title that would be considered politically correct in today's current climate, but Smith, on his day, had run most full backs into the ground and had only recently returned to the Easter Road side after breaking a leg but the old speed, skill and magic was still there.

Another intriguing debut in this game centred on Gerry Baker who, after a teenage tilt with Chelsea, had returned north to Motherwell.

Manager Willie Reid had need for a speedy frontman, Baker filled the bill on the back of a £2,000 transfer fee to Bobby Ancell's Fir Park men.

This particular debut for Baker was intriguing in that he would be in opposition to his younger brother Joe.

After being born in Liverpool in 1940, the family moved north with Joe's embryonic football career being fashioned on the junior scene with Coltness United and Armadale Thistle.

Despite his now rich Lanarkshire accent, the England national selectors remembered his birthplace and selected him for eight caps that yielded a three-goal return.

As for Gerry, he first saw light of day in New York, with that birthplace giving him the right to earn 16 caps for the USA taking in both the 1966 and 1970 World Cups.

Mrs Baker would have been a right proud mum in that dark and dank November day when, because of the fog and bad light, the game began a few minutes early with Saints kicking off towards the Love Street end.

It is not often that the St Mirren faithful take such an immediate liking to a newcomer, but there was no disputing the warmth of the reception they gave the American born Gerry after a lively display up front that the fans had not seen for some time. He ran about with such purpose that he tore holes in the Hibernian rearguard.

St Mirren forced the first corner and from it Gerry Baker drove in a shot that keeper Lawrie Leslie managed to stop - with his face!

With 15 minutes gone Gerry Baker had more bad luck.

Taking a pass from Tommy Bryceland, he cracked in a first time shot, but the ball rebounded off the falling keeper - no wonder the Saints Baker boy scratched his head in perplexity.

St Mirren were lucky not to concede a penalty when Davie Lapsley's size 10s impeded the flying Willie Ormond, but the referee waved play on.

It wasn't all Gerry Baker and St Mirren in the first half. Hibs Joe Baker was also a force to be reckoned with. And he was equally unlucky when he powered in a header, but straight at keeper Campbell Forsyth.

Thoughts on a no scoring first half were providing a positive accolade for fellow debutant Ian Riddell.

He showed no sign of nerves in trying to neutralise the wiles of Hibs Smith.

The winger tended to wander, forsaking his touchline beat, but Riddell was a problem for the Hibs icon.

Three minutes after the break St Mirren forced a corner. Laird sent over the flag kick, Gerry Baker headed it on and Campbell thundered the ball into the net.

Seven minutes later cue a thunderous roar to herald Gerry Baker's first St Mirren goal. He beat centre half Jackie Plenderleith, slipped the ball to Campbell and was in position again to head home the winger's lob to the far post.

Outmanoeuvred and generally caught sitting on their heels for a long spell, Hibernian eventually came back into the game in the 63rd minute with Desmond Fox heading home to reduce the Edinburgh side's leeway.

It wasn't all sweetness and light for the Buddies new livewire front man. Gerry took a bad knock and for a while had to limp along on the left touch line.

There were some anxious moments for the home fans in and around goalkeeper Forsyth's box as Hibernian fought to pull the game out of the fire. And, with the St Mirren youngsters tiring, Hibs held the initiative but couldn't beat the big Saints keeper.

Five minutes from time the Buddies fought back and

MATCH OF THE DAY

Campbell had the ball in the net again only to be ruled offside.

With brother Gerry the hero, with effectively the winning goal and claiming the bragging rights, that evening meal in the Baker household must have been a tenuous occasion with Mrs Baker no doubt stretched to keep the peace.

Teams:

St Mirren: *Forsyth, Lapsley, Riddell, Doonan, McGugan, Gregal, Flynn, Bryceland, Baker, Laird and Campbell.*

Hibernian: *Leslie, Grant, McLelland, Turnbull. Plenderleith, Preston, Smith, Fox, Baker, Aitken and Ormond.*

Referee: *J.R. Barclay (Kirkcaldy).*

Estimated Attendance: *8,000.*

Kick-off: *2.30 pm.*

Davie Lapsley

ST MIRREN 10   PEEBLES ROVERS 0

Scottish Cup 2nd Round

13th February 1959

UESTION - how on earth can you classify this Scottish Cup tie as one of St Mirren's classic matches? Well Peebles Rovers are a well-respected member of the Scottish East of Scotland League and have every right to contest the Scottish Cup.

Founded in 1894, they have a long and competitive history with their neat and tidy Whitestone Park accommodating some 3,000 fans with seating for 500 fans.

What must have been uppermost in the minds of the travelling Rovers fans was this wasn't their first Cup visit to Love Street. In the 1st Round of the 1934-35 competition they had lost 3-1, so would they be able to improve on that scoreline?

There were other facets that were clearly stacked against the wee Rovers. This was the first Scottish Cup match to be played on a Friday night and what was more - this was Friday the 13th.

Further strange conditions awaited Peebles as this was the first match to be played under floodlights at St Mirren Park.

One would have to admit that the lights were still in the embryonic stage, however, with the promise of other lights being added the illumination aspects could only improve.

What was intriguing was the pre-match conversation piece between skipper Davie Lapsley and manager Willie Reid. One can just imagine Lapsley's couthy, Camelon accent.

Lapsley commented: 'Ah jest said to the manager Willie Reid, whit likes the bonus tonight boss?' Willie told me he'd put us on 10/- a goal (or 50p in new money). So I told the boys to score as many as they could.

He would later say: 'So they rattled in ten. That was a fiver on top of their wages, but the wages were only sweeties at that time.'

Pre-match team news saw Davie Walker, only recently joined from Airdrieonians, taking over from Campbell Forsyth in goal. The local Paisley impressions were that Forsyth had not been at his best of late.

In defence Johnny McTurk took over from Ian Riddell otherwise this was the same side that had beaten Clyde at Shawfield in Saints last match. This meant that Jim Rodger and Bobby Holmes would be the St Mirren wingers.

The La Scala cinema was doing big business with 'Around the World in 80 days' - no doubt a possible outing for St Mirren players having no game the following day.

Alternatively, a night in front of the TV might have seduced the senses in watching 'Dixon of Dock Green' or, 'The Black & White Minstrel Show.'

Peebles came to Love Street, saw St Mirren at their best and were promptly thrashed with a double figure scoreline.

Just in case anyone thought this was a humiliating outing for the East of Scotland side, they can be assured this Rovers team were delighted - they went home the richer by more than £400.

Players and fans alike were suitably impressed with the quality of the floodlighting. Yes, there were a few dark patches, but a further 14 lamps would be fitted prior to the game with Dunfermline in five days' time.

It was a pointless task to analyse the game. Keeper Davie Walker didn't have a shot to save while the defensive trio of Lapsley, McTurk and McGugan didn't need to break sweat.

St Mirren, by playing with the front foot firmly on the accelerator pedal, gave the crowd their money's worth and in Jackie Neilson, Gerry Baker and Tommy Bryceland, Saints had the night's stars.

When the final whistle sounded both sets of players held back to let the Peebles keeper Brunton go in first - he turned in a brilliant display and deserved the honour.

Baker, Gemmell and Bryceland all had scoring attempts before Baker opened the scoring in the 20th minute heading home a Rodger cross with Gerry adding a second four minutes later.

An amazing stushie took place midway through the first half right on the Rovers goal line, but although almost virtually every St Mirren player tried, they couldn't force the ball home.

Baker did two minutes later, nodding in another Rodger cross for his hat trick with Bryceland making it 4-0 at the interval.

Brunton was performing heroics in the Rovers goal but couldn't prevent Bryceland adding a fifth and in the 55th minute Baker drove in his fourth.

Holmes made it seven up in scoring his first for the senior side after a barren two-year break. Midway through the half Rodger danced round the keeper to score number eight.

After 77 minutes Holmes made it nine with the Bryceland fella, just on the final whistle, making it a double figure scoreline.

Teams:
St Mirren: *Walker, Lapsley, McTurk, Neilson, McGugan, Gregal, Rodger, Bryceland, Baker, Gemmell and Holmes.*
Peebles Rovers: *Brunton, Burgess, Blyth, Hogg, Brown, Howieson, Hailstones, Nicol, Miller, Harvey and Reid.*
Referee: *R. Morrow (Falkirk).*
Attendance: *8,085.*
Drawings: *£891. 7. 6.*

Tommy Gemmell

CELTIC 0 ST MIRREN 4

Scottish Cup Semi-Final

4th April 1959

THE route to the later stages of the 1959 Scottish Cup campaign weighed heavily in St Mirren's favour.

A decisive 2nd Round home win over non-league Peebles Rovers was followed by another home 3-2 win over Motherwell.

Things were becoming tasty with yet another home tie this time lowering the colours of Dunfermline at the quarter final stage.

While Aberdeen and the late lamented Third Lanark fought out one semi-final at Ibrox, St Mirren faced Celtic at Hampden in the other.

This was the era when clubs were happy to wear their own registered strips without having the occasional need for an 'away' outfit.

St Mirren wore their familiar vertical striped shirts with

Celtic donning their traditional horizontal hoops.

Both wore white shorts and neither team had any problems with visual or identification confusion.

The only confusion around was who was this mediocre team that the Buddies were playing? This game with its final scoreline was in effect skittle alley!

Saints exhibited a cockiness that had to be seen to be believed.

They tore the renowned Celtic half back line apart while the Love Street defenders treated the Parkhead forward line with disdain and contempt.

St Mirren led 3-0 at the interval and all against a particularly boisterous wind.

On reflection the only thing that Celtic won was the toss!

While Celtic huffed and puffed, St Mirren hadn't a failure. Obviously this Saintly bunch of lads from Paisley hadn't read the betting odds.

If someone had told them Celts were 6-4 on and St Mirren were being offered at 5-2 against, they would have raised their eyes in mock horror.

Frank Haffey pulled off a superb save to deny Saints before the Hoops did find the net, but winger John Divers was adjudged offside.

St Mirren were bubbling with crisp inter passing in some style, the accuracy of their passes causing severe mayhem in the Parkhead goalmouth.

St Mirren's flair for the unexpected created their first goal.

A long punt from keeper David Walker found Alistair Miller free on the left touchline. An interchange between Miller, Tommy Gemmell and Jim Rodger found the former still running full pelt.

He then rounded Bobby Evans to drive an unstoppable rocket past Haffey. Time 16 minutes.

The know-all pundits were ecstatic - so were the travelling Paisley support - there has never been a finer goal in a Hampden semi.

One didn't know at the time, but on reflection this was the beginning of the end for those clad in green and white.

Celtic did manage a sortie or two into the Saints box. But, what materialised was pinball stuff with any port in a storm being the cry to keep the Saints goal intact.

Bobby Evans was becoming sick at the futility of his forward line. He lost the place, tried to take on the St Mirren defence on his own, was dispossessed and stranded leaving acres of space in the Celtic rearguard.

Miller and wee Gemmell said thank you very much, knitted a pattern of supreme passing skills allowing the mercurial Miller to round Haffey and deposit number two in the empty net. Time 33 minutes.

Flying Celtic winger Sammy Wilson then proceeded to demonstrate that this wasn't Celtic's day when he mis-headed a ball straight to the educated feet of Rodger. The winger made tracks and crossed a beauty for Gerry Baker to diddle Evans and run on to shoot past the now thoroughly despondent Haffey. Time 38 minutes.

The second half was a virtual walk for Saints, happy to retain possession and cause the residents of Celtic Park to run around like a bunch of headless chickens.

Still Saints weren't finished and rubbed salt into the ever-growing Celtic wounds when Jackie Neilson lobbed in a ball to the far post in the last minute where Bryceland took a rebound from the keeper to score Saints fourth.

The Man of the Match accolade had many contenders, nearly all in black and white, but few would dispute the honour going to Saints flying winger Alistair Miller.

This was a classic display by St Mirren the only pity being that at a ground with a capacity of over 130,000, there wasn't a bigger crowd to appreciate the St Mirren finesse.

Teams:
Celtic: *Haffey, Mackay, Mochan, Smith, Evans, Peacock, McVittie, Jackson, Lochhead, Wilson and Divers.*
St Mirren: *Walker, Lapsley, Wilson, Neilson, McGugan, Leishman, Rodger, Bryceland, Baker, Gemmell and Miller.*
Referee: *R.H. Davidson.*
Attendance: *73,885.*

Jackie Neilson

ST MIRREN 3   ABERDEEN 1

Scottish Cup Final

25th April 1959

EVERAL questions were being posted prior to this game, which was St Mirren's fourth final attempt at landing the coveted silverware, although they had achieved success in collecting the trophy way back in 1926 with a 2-0 win over Celtic.

Would the Saints succeed in overcoming the 33-year wait in assuaging their Scottish Cup Final thirst?

Would the Paisley and District public turn out and offer their support?

Would Gerry Baker manage another goal? After all, he had scored in every other round of this season's competition.

All such queries were positively answered in the affirmative.

And, in particular, Paisley and District's contribution to the amazing attendance of 108,591 was prodigious in the extreme.

It was estimated that approximately 60,000 had created an exodus of biblical proportions from the town en route for Hampden Park.

Seven special trains left St James and Gilmour Street stations with over 300 buses and countless cars making the journey to the Mount Florida venue.

St Mirren were clearly up for the game being first out onto the pitch some three or four minutes ahead of Aberdeen. Davie Lapsley lost the toss with the Dons skipper Archie Glen opting for the Pittodrie side kicking off towards the Mount Florida end.

As expected, the early play became a mite feisty with referee Jack Mowat having to offer words of a cautionary gesture to both Glen for taking out Tommy Bryceland, then for Baker's overly robust challenge on Jim Clunie.

The Aberdeen game plan effectively stymied the Saints inside forward trio and it was left to Baker's speed to capitalise on any openings, but the best of the chances were created by the long through balls from Jackie Neilson and Tommy Leishman.

The Aberdeen trainer was a busy man having firstly to attend to full back Caldwell, who was off the field for a while with his position going to, of all people, wing man Jackie Hather.

Big Clunie then required some running repairs after a one-on-one joust with Bryceland.

Four minutes prior to the break Saints passed up a glorious chance to open the scoring.

Baker made an opening for Jim Rodger, but the best he could conjure up was a corner with both Miller and Baker in space and shrieking for a return pass.

Saints weren't to be denied and the breakthrough came just a couple of minutes from the interval.

Wee Bryceland, he of the baggy shorts, rose to beat keeper Fred Martin all ends up with a magnificent header. That goal was virtually a carbon copy of the winning header that Bobby Charlton scored against Scotland at Wembley a fortnight earlier.

One up at the interval, the Saints fans were pretty

pleased with themselves and the half time pies and Bovril were being consumed with great gusto.

Aberdeen resumed with Caldwell, still limping on the left wing from injury. And he missed a great opportunity to give the Dons parity.

Davie Walker was beaten by a cross from the right and Caldwell hobbled in to turn the ball just past the post. Lucky Saints!

It was all non-stop St Mirren hereabouts.

Tommy Leishman hit a piledriver that all but shattered the cross bar. Jackie Neilson followed, smashing a great shot just over and Jim Rodger, not to be left out, fired in a shot that Fred Martin did well to touch over.

By now the Granite City team were pretty groggy. Mis-timed tackles were now the order of the day with whistler Mowat keeping the lid on things in booking St Mirren's 'Cockles' Wilson and Baker as well Norman Davidson of Aberdeen.

The Dons defence were immense in repelling the repeated St Mirren attacks, but they cracked in the 63rd minute.

Neilson was the soccer engineer with a magnificent through pass to Tommy Gemmell who twice crashed shots against Martin's not inconsiderable frame. The second of these ran along the goal line for Alistair Miller to simply tap home. As Milles was prone to remind folk - he was lethal from one yard!

By now the rain had been coming down pretty steadily, but it didn't in any way dampen the enthusiasm of the Paisley faithful.

If they had to salvage anything from this game, Aberdeen had to take it towards the Saints goal and, as happens on such situations, left themselves exposed at the back.

The execution axe came down on the Aberdeen necks in the 77th minute.

Bryceland was the instigator in slipping a neat pass to Baker who whipped in a drive well out of Martin's reach. Baker had fulfilled the Paisley expectations in scoring in every round - he was mobbed by his ecstatic team mates.

The Dons reorganised their set up with Clunie taking on

the centre forward role, but by now Saints were way out in front and were effectively running down the clock.

Baker wasn't finished though, four minutes from time he streaked past Glen now at centre half, but only succeeded in lofting the ball over the bar. The Baker hair was torn in mortal anguish.

Bryceland, with one final mickey taking gesture, put the ball in the Aberdeen net but was clearly offside. With almost the last kick of the game Baird scored a consolation goal for the Dons.

After the final whistle cue bedlam. Thousands of Paisley's finest jumped the perimeter walls and rushed onto the field dodging the attentions of the thin - very thin - blue constabulary line.

The St Mirren players were jubilant with Davie Lapsley leading his troops to lift the cup. The Aberdeen lads were pretty despondent but none more so than inside right Norman Davidson.

He too was also in line to score in every round but that particular accolade was the sole possession of Saints' American-born flyer Gerry Baker.

There was one additional postscript to this game.

After winning the cup in 1926 each of the winning St Mirren players was presented with a bottle of whisky.

Goal scorer on that occasion, Davie McCrae, put his bottle into cold storage vowing not to open it until St Mirren next won the cup.

His intent was fulfilled when in the company of TV commentator Arthur Montford, the bottle was ceremoniously opened with Davie Lapsley the recipient of the first dram.

Teams:

St Mirren: *Walker, Lapsley, Wilson. Neilson, McGugan. Leishman, Rodger, Bryceland, Baker, Gemmell and Miller.*

Aberdeen: *Martin, Caldwell, Hogg, Brownlie, Clunie, Glen, Ewen, Davidson, Baird, Wishart and Hather.*

Referee: *Mr J.A. Mowat, Burnside.*

Attendance: *108,591.*

Gerry Baker

ST MIRREN 15   GLASGOW UNIVERSITY 0

Scottish Cup - 1st Round

30th January 1960

 HE last January Saturday in 1960 saw Paisley under siege by garishly garbed gangs of students seeking to relieve you of any loose change in support of their annual Students' Charity Day.

Many charitable associates belonged to the Philip McCann tribe while many Arabs, sporting tea towel turbans, demanded your very last shekel.

There were other students in town that day wearing a uniform of black and gold; these were the footballing lambs of Glasgow University that were fed meekly to the St Mirren slaughter house that was called, indecently on this occasion, Love Street.

This was a game abundant in records. American born Gerry Baker, who had seemed to have lost the Midas touch for goal-getting in recent games, recaptured his 'goalden' touch when he rattled ten into the Glasgow students' 'tinney' to equal a 20th century British record.

It was Joe Payne who was the first to fire in 10 in a Division Three league match for Luton Town against Bristol Rovers on April 13th 1936. Clearly it was John Petrie who topped the all-time scoring records when he netted 13 for Arbroath in that 36-0 walloping of Bon Accord back in September 1885.

Certainly Baker's 10, and the overall 15 for the club, were both new St Mirren records. In the 1920s, St Mirren had an Englishman - Terry Wagner - at centre forward who scored seven in one game and this is believed to have been the previous best.

If St Mirren's skill factor was going to be a problem for the 'Yoonie', they had an even bigger hurdle to contend with in the atrocious weather conditions. It was blowing a gale with driving sleet and snow in close attendance.

St Mirren kicked off into the wind and snow towards the Love Street end. The sympathetic Saints crowd raised the decibel ratings for the students as they occasionally took the play towards Davie Walker's goal.

Every time a student beat a St Mirren player the crowd voiced their support and in forcing a corner in the 12th minute the Glasgow boys almost earned a standing ovation.

The young student left winger Finlayson, a Paisley engineering student, was perhaps the only one to showcase any soccer panache. A bright future was predicted for him as and when he might forsake the amateur ranks for the pro stage.

It took Saints 25 minutes to open the scoring, Ian Riddell and Alistair Miller orchestrated a move down the left wing and when the cross came over Baker was on hand to apply the coup de grace.

After the half hour mark Baker put the Saints two up when he took a pass from Riddell to drive home from 12 yards.

A minute later Baker notched his hat trick nodding home from close range. Just a minute from the sanctuary of a warm dressing room, Baker hit home number four to make the half time scoreline Gerry Baker 4 Glasgow University 0.

A minute after the restart goalkeeper Saltrese got himself into a bit of a granny knot with his defence allowing Baker to tap home.

Baker scored number six after 54 minutes, taking a pass from Tommy Bryceland to manufacture a brilliant solo goal. A minute later wee Tommy Gemmell supplied the ammunition for Baker's and St Mirren's seventh while No 8 arrived courtesy of a Jackie McGugan corner, which Baker deflected home.

By now the weather conditions were taking their toll on the part time students who were tiring rapidly, in fact they had great difficulty in clearing the ball out of their own area.

Gemmell broke the scoring sequence slotting home the ninth and tenth goals, full back Tait deflecting home the second. On 75 minutes and three minutes later Baker was at it again netting numbers 11 and 12.

That 12th goal was the one that remains the most memorable in Baker's memory banks.

He recalled, 'A corner came over from the left, their keeper went for it and I went for it. He opted to clear the ball with a winder that crashed off me in a very masculine area.

'In fact, it promptly transfigured me from being a blossoming baritone to a screaming soprano!

'The trainer Jimmy McGarvey took me off the field and even tried to persuade me to go back on as there was still 12 minutes to go. But I was freezing cold and had had enough. I just wanted into that hot bath!'

The final scoring run saw the last three goals coming from Jack McGugan, Jim Rodger and Miller with the latter, in his usual irrepressible way, maintaining that it was his goal that sealed the win.

One newspaper postscript summed up the landslide victory saying: 'Bryceland and Gemmell were the male nurses in an operating theatre, where Gerry Baker was the surgeon who amputated the 'Yoonie' students' dream of cup glory.'

Teams:

St Mirren: *Walker, McTurk, Wilson, McGugan, Tierney, Riddell, Rodger, Bryceland, Baker, Gemmell and Miller.*

Glasgow University: *N. Saltrese, N. Purdie, R. Tait, N. Alexander, R. Ramage, I. Strangeways, G. Kirk, A. Small, D. Forrest, A. McNiven and A. Finlayson.*

Referee: *J. Mackie, East Kilbride.*

Attendance: *7,449*

Gate: *£781 14s 6d.*

Cathkin Park

THIRD LANARK 0   ST MIRREN 8

Scottish Cup 3rd Round Replay

28th February 1961

T O appreciate the full theatre of this remarkable result, one has to revert to the match that created the replay at Love Street.

Third Lanark came calling having met Saints on Scottish Cup duty on 16 previous occasions with the scoreline pendulum swinging in St Mirren's favour with seven wins and seven draws.

This Third Lanark side were a formidable team with a ferocious goal appetite. In that 1960-61 season they posted exactly 100 league goals, the nearest to them being the League champions Rangers with a mere 88.

Some of the Cathkin Park side's scoring exploits were phenomenal, scoring a five and a six on each of three occasions, they even managed to net seven against Clyde.

Front-runners for this goal machine were Dave Hilley and Alex Harley. Indeed, these two were on target to give Thirds a 2-1 lead in the original cup tie with Big Jim Clunie converting a penalty for Saints after John McCormack had decked the mercurial Donnie Kerrigan in the box.

Tommy Bryceland netted the Saints equaliser in the second half, but Paisley hopes became somewhat threadbare and anxious when wee Joe McInnes cottoned on to the rebound after an Alex Harley strike rattled off the bar to score with only nine minutes left. Cue right-half, Rab Stewart, the man whose single goal had disposed of Dundee United in the previous round.

Only three minutes to go and Saints force a corner from the left. As it came over it broke to Stewart whose pile driver zoomed past the diminutive Jocky Robertson. Three each, a fantastic game, the Saints fans revelling in the euphoria and so on to Cathkin for the replay.

A crowd of 20,893 paying £1,650 turned out to see a slice of football history at Cathkin Park.

Never in the annals of the Scottish Cup has a First Division club, after forcing a replay on their home patch, gone on to annihilate the opposition on their ground in the manner of St Mirren's turnover of Third Lanark.

Saints were two up at the coffee break.

Tommy Bryceland hit a belter for the first after Jim Rodger had out jumped the Cathkin skipper Jim Reilly. Donnie Kerrigan netted number two, taking a pass from Alistair Miller to meander through the Thirds defence to beat Jocky Robertson. Only two down, Third Lanark still had a chance.

They came on strongly in the second period, but Jim Clunie was immense in marshalling the St Mirren rearguard.

The Cathkin deflation started in the 59th minute with Rodger scoring a simple goal with the Third Lanark defence being AWOL.

Minutes later Rodger burst through the home rearguard to net number four with a pile driver. A fifth goal followed with a special from Alistair Miller, who always reckoned he was deadly from two yards - these were his words!

By now Rodger had swapped places with Donnie Kerrigan. Kerrigan had sustained an injury and went on to hirple on the right wing - these being the days before the introduction of substitutes. Jim took to his new centre forward role by slamming home number six to complete his hat trick.

He went on to score Saints seventh and his own fourth before Bryceland ended the rout with the eighth. It was a remarkable achievement and a fantastic quartet of goals for Rodger.

Rodger has often been asked as to which of his goals was the most memorable for him.

He said, 'I think it would have to be the fourth and the seventh for the team. As you know by now I was operating in the centre forward role due to Donnie Kerrigan's slight injury.

'I took a ball about 35 or 40 yards out and went at the now stricken Thirds defence who kept backing off. 'Tackle him, tackle him' they shouted.

'When I got to the 20-yard mark I hit a left foot shot with a wee bit of a curl on it and it veered way past Jocky Robertson and flew into the top left hand corner.'

The thoughts down Love Street way generated visions of cup silverware landing in the boardroom show case after this momentous win. Would it happen? There was a modicum of momentum in the 4th Round when Hearts were beaten 1-0 at Tynecastle thanks to a Kerrigan goal.

It was Tynecastle again for the semi-final against Dunfermline and a scoreless result. But back at Tynecastle, our replay technology was found wanting with the East End Park side going 1-0. Clearly it was the Pars who had mastered this replay activity beating Celtic in the final after a re-run under the shrewd guidance of Jock Stein.

Teams:

Third Lanark: *Robertson, McGilvray, Caldwell, Reilly, McCormack, Lewis, Goodfellow, Hilley, Harley, Gray and McInnes.*

St Mirren: *Brown, Campbell, Wilson, Stewart, Clunie, Riddell, Rodger, Bryceland, Kerrigan, McTavish and Miller.*

Referee: R.H. Davidson (Airdrie)

Attendance: 20,000

Tottie Beck

ST MIRREN 5   RAITH ROVERS 1

Division One

20th January 1962

AINTS were in a bit of a quandary - the players' win bonuses had become conspicuous by their absence.

It was way back in late November when the full points had last been garnered in a game at Muirton Park against St Johnstone thanks to strikes from Donnie Kerrigan, Therolf Beck and Willie Fernie in a 3-0 win.

Bobby Flavell had taken over the management reins before Christmas after the seven-year reign of Willie Reid. However, Flavell hadn't as yet even tasted a single win.

Team confidence was at a low ebb, not surprisingly after a 7-0 gubbing at the hands of Dunfermline, at East End Park, in late December.

A clutch of postponed games heralded the start of January with Kilmarnock arriving midweek on 17th January.

Some semblance of confidence returned with the Saints

recording a 2-1 win thanks to the sprightly Tommy Henderson and Jim McDonald the marksmen on the day. McDonald's goal arriving just five minutes from time.

That confidence factor zoomed to the surface in the match with Raith Rovers three days later in no small way due to the terrible twosome, as the media were prone to label wee Tommy Henderson and 'Tottie' Beck, the pair tormenting and terrorising the Stark's Park men big time.

It wasn't surprising that the North Bank patrons found some vocal difficulties in bestowing praise on someone called Therolf, so Tottie was much more meaningful in bestowing friendly appraisal.

Tottie Beck had been a smash hit in his native Iceland and in a pre-season match in Reykjavik, the visiting St Mirren team had succumbed to a 7-1 turn over with this blonde Adonis called Beck scoring a hat-trick.

He had potential and once the red tape had been unravelled Beck signed for St Mirren and made his debut against Airdrie at Love Street on October 21st - and he hit the goal trail running by scoring four in his first six matches.

For a while the goals dried up and some pundits were prone to label Beck as being found wanting and too gentle for the rumbustious Scottish game.

But, come this Raith Rovers game, he certainly stood up to be counted in this men's game to prove his point.

The diminutive Henderson, a pint sized winger from Hearts, was manager Flavell's first signing and in this 5-1 win over the Kirkcaldy side, while it was Beck who supplied the finishing touches, it was Henderson who supplied the build up ammunition.

The first half was virtually conducted at a walking pace and although St Mirren went in for the half-time cuppa one-up, they should have scored half-a-dozen.

It was on the resumption that Henderson rolled his stockings down to boot level in the same style as Tommy Bryceland used to do and, for want of a more articulate expression, simply 'Got stuck in!'

Back to the match beginning and the St Mirren forwards were combining well and in one early sortie Willie Fernie took the ball for a walk and hammered in a shot that went wide when a pass to the unmarked Beck would have earned a more profitable return.

Raith Rovers lost Andy Leigh after a tackle from, of all people Henderson, and had to leave the field for some extensive treatment.

Saints deservedly took the lead on the half hour mark.

Stewart created the opening with a pass to Willie Fernie who headed for the bye-line to cut the ball back for Beck to beat the future St Mirren goalkeeper Jim Thorburn with a crisp shot.

Just seconds before the break Alistair Miller had the ball in the net, but was penalised for offside.

Andy Leigh returned after the interval following considerable treatment. However, he was limited to a limping role on the left touchline.

The home side were squandering chances galore in this game more than they might expect to get in half-a-dozen games or so.

Then came the turning point.

On the hour mark, Beck put St Mirren further ahead, but the Raith players en masse protested vehemently that the Icelander was offside. However, the goal stood.

The Saints were now on song in converting their opportunities and Beck turned provider for George McLean to smash home number three.

By now St Mirren were coasting to the two points and McLean repaid the creativity factor to Beck who added the fourth and thus celebrated his hat trick.

Straight from the kick off, Raith Rovers reduced the leeway when Watson hammered in a pile driver that zoomed past Jimmy Brown in the Saints goal. Time 76 minutes.

Clearly with his guile, trickery and speed Henderson was virtually the Man of the Match, but that accolade went to Beck who, seven minutes from the final whistle, latched on

to a rebound from George McLean to net his fourth and make the final scoreline 5-1.

Many iconic Saints have scored a quartet of the best; one remembers the four goals by Jim Rodger in the Third Lanark replay, Gerry Burrell netting four against Morton and Alex Crowe with his contribution against Hearts. However, for this particular season, and experiencing a goal drought, Beck's return was more than welcome.

Teams:

St Mirren: *Brown, Doonan, Wilson, Stewart, Clunie, McTavish, Henderson, McLean, Beck, Fernie and Miller.*

Raith Rovers: *Thorburn, Wilson, Mochan, Stein, Forsyth, Leigh, Benvie, White, Price, Malcolm and Watson.*

Referee: *A.J.T. Cook, Edinburgh.*

Estimated Attendance: *8,000.*

Willie Fernie

CELTIC 1 ST MIRREN 3

Scottish Cup semi-final

31st March 1962

HAT constitutes a classic game? High quality of the soccer skills on show? Perhaps a game with a sense of occasion? Maybe your team coming out on top after being labelled as the underdogs?

Or, is it a match where winning heralds a degree of progression in a particular competition?

All these aspects were applicable to St Mirren in this Scottish Cup semi-final against Celtic at Ibrox Stadium.

However, if these were plus points - there was one high negative cloud that engulfed the game. Read on...

Five days earlier St Mirren had played Celtic in a rearranged league encounter at Love Street when the home team was severely whipped courtesy of a 0-5 scoreline.

And to digest such a result on the back of successive 3-1 defeats at the hands of St Johnstone and Airdrie, inevitably the confidence factor in again facing the Parkhead side at Ibrox was plummeting zero-wards.

Manager Bobby Flavell made wholesale changes for the cup tie.

He did persevere with Bobby Williamson in goal, which proved to be masterstroke ,with the former Arbroath keeper providing heroics between the St Mirren sticks.

Either owing to injury, or to a loss of form out went John McTavish, Jackie Neilson, Alistair Miller, Tommy Gemmell and Jim McDonald to be replaced by Stewart, McLean, Donnie Kerrigan, Tottie Beck and Campbell.

Tommy Bryceland was a last minute inclusion, although the Greenock-born wizard wasn't 100% fit.

Celtic won the toss with St Mirren kicking off and enjoying a stiff breeze on their backs. In the early stages keeper Frank Haffey was a lucky man not to be beaten by the energetic Beck as the Icelander's lob was net bound only to be cleared off the line by full back Kennedy.

But Saints were not to be denied and it took them only eight minutes to open their account. Beck made the opening for the diminutive Tommy Henderson to fire in a cross, but a Haffey fumble saw Fifer Willie Fernie on hand to pilot the loose ball over the line.

One up and, after the previous Monday's debacle, the Paisley fans were warming to this scoreline with increasing volumes of their local national anthems.

Little had been seen of Tommy Bryceland, he seemed to be pacing himself for a full 90-minute shift.

Then came the first touch of the Bryceland magic. He danced past three Celts only to be flattened in the box by Paddy Crerand.

The tackling was tough, but deemed perfectly legal by Mr MacKenzie.

When 32 minutes had passed, St Mirren went further head.

Beck fashioned a through ball for Kerrigan to race after and the Saints centre forward nearly burst the onion bag with a pile driver.

Just 60 seconds later Beck was again on hand to take a defence splitting pass from Henderson to knock in number three. Three up at the break, this was classic history in the making.

Celtic, now with the wind in their favour, began to exert a modicum of pressure. But Williamson produced a string of saves in the supreme quality category to keep the Hoops at bay.

Midway through the second period, the natives garbed in a selection of green and white favours, were becoming restless with the perceived vision of a place in the final starting to recede at a fast rate of knots.

A number of fights broke out on the Copland Road terracing behind Williamson's goal.

Bottles flew as hundreds of spectators crowded onto the pitch. This intrusion triggered a reaction from the other end of the ground as thousands invaded the playing area in an endeavour to have the game stopped.

By now the referee had stopped the play and taken the players off.

Saints manager Flavell went berserk thinking that the game had been abandoned, as had the Celtic support.

However, Strathclyde's finest thought otherwise.

It took another eight minutes to clear the pitch with Mr MacKenzie bringing the players back on call for the final 15 minutes.

Some consolation - not a lot - came Celtic's way three minutes from time when Hughes and Chalmers combined to give winger Byrne a consolation goal.

For Celtic and St Mirren, two great institutions in the Scottish game and both founder members of the Scottish League, it is regrettable that when all else is forgotten, Saints' 3-1 classic win will not be remembered for the Love Street club's stylish play but for the disgrace of the Ibrox riot.

In the summary of who did what and who did well, Bobby Williamson was immense in goal with the keeper staging one of the finest displays of the goalkeeping art while

Campbell, Wilson and Clunie all earned Great Saints status.

A word in praise of the St Mirren fans.

They remained calm in the face of a crisis as they cheered they team to a victory - a victory that few expected, but one that was fully deserved.

Postscript: A place in the final against Rangers had now been achieved with the possibility of a money-spinning run in the European Cup-Winners' Cup tourney. Alas that was an unfulfilled dream losing out 2-0 to the Ibrox club in the final.

Teams:

Celtic: *Haffey, McKay, Kennedy, Crerand, McNeil, Clark, Brogan, Chalmers, Hughes, Divers and Byrne.*

St Mirren: *Williamson, Campbell, Wilson, Stewart, Clunie, McLean, Henderson, Bryceland, Kerrigan, Fernie and Beck.*

Referee: *A. MacKenzie, Coatbridge.*

Attendance: *59, 276.*

Jack Copland

ST MIRREN 1   ARBROATH 1

Division Two Title-Winning Match

7th April 1968

THIS was the day. The probability of Division One football for season 1968-69 came to a conclusion - a positive conclusion in this re-arranged Wednesday match - when those with an ear for music might have appropriately enjoyed the classic choral rendering of Sir Hugh Roberton's 'All In An April Evening.'

Arbroath were the Love Street visitors and for most of the season the Red Lichties had been chasing the St Mirren heels with the likelihood that the championship would eventually go to East Fife, Queen's Park or either participants in this game.

Like St Mirren, the Gayfield club also had a mad rush to fulfil their end of season fixtures with seven games to be completed in a 25-day spell.

At the end of that April evening Saints were the champions - but in name only!

The Buddies struggled to their third successive drawn

game at Love Street to take the single point that officially gave them the Division Two title.

More than 5,000 fans turned up to see Saints squash the Arbroath challenge at the top of the table.

If St Mirren failed to produce the expected goods, Arbroath, who now looked set to join St Mirren in Division One, fared hardly any better.

Saints' slump has been evident in their past three games and at times, even in midfield where they had been particularly dominant, they were struggling against the east coast side.

Only for about 15 minutes before the interval did the Love Street lads find their championship form. During this period, they hit Arbroath with everything bar the kitchen sink, but there was no killer punch to finish off the groggy Red Lichties.

There is no doubt the league leaders missed the drive of Peter Kane up front. Jim Blair, normally a sure fire deputy, had a game that was classified as poor by his normally predatory standards.

Former Paisley Grammar School boy Jack Copland was making his debut. The lad had a quiet game, although he did contribute a couple of rocket shots, one of which nearly splintered keeper Williamson's cross bar.

This draw put Arbroath four points clear of Queen's Park and although the Hampden amateurs had a game in hand the Gayfield side now needed only two points from their last two games to join the Saints 'upstairs' the following season.

Goals were conspicuous by their absence and Bobby Pinkerton, who recently had been voted as the St Mirren Player of the Year, twice had the opportunity to open the Saints account but shot past.

He did have one almighty pile driver that was brilliantly saved by Williamson which would surely be in the shortleet for Save of the Season.

The no scoring first half gave the expectant fans the impression that Paisley nerves were eroding away the team's confidence as they chased the Championship winning line.

Skipper Willie Renton took it in his hands to inject some drive and one thunderbolt from all of 30 yards just squirmed past Williamson's upright.

Arbroath weren't out of it and centre forward Jack powered his way through to embarrass Andy McFadden with a nutmeg only to have Jim Thorburn smother the ball at the post.

It took St Mirren 61 minutes to take the lead and even then the goal didn't come from open play.

Tony Connell, the top player on the field, raced into the box but was unceremoniously flattened by Sellars with Cammy Murray accepting the responsibility to drive home the spot kick.

The Paisley cheers were somewhat muted four minutes later when Bruce executed a one-two of supreme quality to drive home the equaliser.

One each secured the championship - cue the champagne and attendant Paisley celebrations.

Postscript: Arbroath did manage to beat both Alloa and Ayr United in their last two games to secure the runner-up spot and promotion, although they were subsequently relegated the following season.

Teams:

St Mirren: *Thorburn, Murray, Connell, Fulton, McFadden, Renton, Duffy, Copland, Blair, Pinkerton and Hamilton. Substitute: McLaughlin.*

Arbroath: *Williamson, Cameron, Hughes, Cargill, Stirling, Kennedy, Sellars, Cant, Jack, Bruce and Wilkie. Substitute: Pierson.*

Referee: *J.W. Paterson (Bothwell).*

Estimated Attendance: *5,000.*

Willie Fulton

ST MIRREN 4   BERWICK RANGERS 0

Division Two Final League Match

29th April 1968

THE final Division Two run-in for season 1967-68 provided a hectic programme for St Mirren.

The only league defeat the Buddies had sustained was by East Fife, back in February, losing 2-1 at Bayview Park.

The Saints were in sight of the title, but were faced with seven games in 19 days to complete their fixture list by the end of April. Their focus remained on winning promotion, with Arbroath, East Fife and Queen's Park their nearest title challengers.

With draws against Montrose and Albion Rovers, one more point would give them the championship, a feat they duly accomplished at the hands of Arbroath (see chapter dated April 17th 1968).

While the euphoria on winning promotion was well milked by the Paisley faithful other targets loomed on the horizon.

With that draw against Arbroath, the Saints' Goals For column registered a total of 83 with four games to go.

It was only after the 'Loons' of Forfar Athletic had been decimated with a 7-0 mauling in the next game at Love Street that any thoughts of achieving a ton-up goal total began to assume the prospects of probability.

After Forfar it was on to Coatbridge's Cliftonhill Stadium where Saints continued on their merry way with a 5-0 thrashing of Albion Rovers. For the Goals For column now read 95.

The penultimate game, a trip to Firs Park to meet up with East Stirlingshire, was the scheduled fixture.

The 'Shire' side were languishing in the lower reaches of the division and the likelihood of a goal harvest seemed a possibility. Not so, the plucky 'Shire side held the Division Two champions to a 1-1 draw - four goals now from the targeted ton-up.

It was the arrival of Berwick Rangers at Love Street that brought congratulations for manager Alex Wright and his ton-up Saints.

With a devastating display, the table toppers ripped the tight Berwick Rangers defence to shreds to notch up the four goals needed to take their league tally to 100.

Every Saint was a hero in this scoring spree, but the man who added the finishing touches to the ammunition supplied regularly from behind was big Jim Blair.

In the 75th minute he sent the Paisley fans wild with joy when he completed his own hat trick and scored that all important 100th goal with a raging shot into the roof of the net.

The green sward of Love Street suddenly became a sea of black and white as hundreds of young St Mirren fans swarmed onto the pitch to acclaim their team.

Right from the whistle the Buddies made it clear their prime objective was to reach that century accolade and the home fans responded as the Saints piled on the pressure.

Some of St Mirren's home displays have been found wanting. Not so on this showing.

Without doubt they had reserved their finest display of the campaign for this final outing.

Berwick seldom looked dangerous but their spasmodic raids never found the St Mirren defence wanting.

With Willie Fulton in imperious form as a sweeper, defensively, the Saints had nothing to fear.

The wing half had his finest outing in a black and white shirt and didn't waste a single ball throughout the 90 minutes.

Other top defenders were Andy McFadden and Tony Connell who both coasted through the game. Team skipper Willie Renton covered a lot of acreage and at times produced some brilliant touches. Only the woodwork and some wonder saves by keeper Jock Wallace prevented him from getting his name on the score sheet.

Yes, it was the same Jock Wallace who went on to manage both Motherwell and Rangers.

In attack Hugh McLaughlin chased everything as though his life depended on it.

Three-goal Jim Blair looked out of touch early on, but went on to show why his goal grabbing expertise had generated a £5,000 transfer tag round his neck.

Jimmy Adamson, Bobby Pinkerton and Ronnie Hamilton all contributed industrious performances, although 'Pinkie' was marginally out of touch with his finishing.

Jim Thorburn celebrated his 36th league game of the season with an incredible 19 shut outs. The keeper had an impressive season with a 100% appearance record in all games. In truth he could not afford to miss a game, as for most of the season he was the only keeper on the St Mirren books.

Saints went on the attack from the opening whistle and in 16 minutes the pressure paid off with Blair intercepting a wayward pass-back to Wallace to put St Mirren ahead.

Five minutes later Blair was at it again. Connell and Hamilton were the providers leaving Big Jim to beat Wallace with some style.

Two goals up at the break, St Mirren shot out of the traps

seeking their 99th and 100th goals.

The first came from Hamilton who blasted home with Blair providing the icing on the cake with the combination of his hat trick and goal number 100.

Teams:

St Mirren: *Thorburn, Murray, Connell, Fulton, McFadden, Renton, Adamson, Pinkerton, McLaughlin, Blair and Hamilton. Substitute: Duffy.*

Berwick Rangers: *Wallace, Paterson, Haig, Markland, Coutts, Smith, Kennedy, Hamilton, Dowds, Brown and Lillie. Substitute: Tait.*

Referee: *J.H. McKee (Kirkintilloch).*

Estimated Attendance: *2,500.*

Alex Ferguson

DUNDEE 0 ST MIRREN 4

Division 1

19th April 1977

HILE promotion occasions can generate wild days of celebration, fortunately in the long history of St Mirren Football Club there haven't been too many relegation induced games logged into the club archives.

Saints were a top division club from the inaugural Scottish League in 1890-91 until 1934-35.

Their tenure in Division Two then lasted a mere twelve months before they returned to the top grade.

A further 31 years elapsed before relegation again struck Paisley's finest and again the lower league participation lasted only a year with manager Alex Wright's team climbing back up the promotion stairs to Division One in 1968.

Relegation again reared its ugly head in 1970-71 and it took the managerial magic of Alex Ferguson to steer the

Buddies, hungry for the Division One menu, back into the top flight in 1976-77.

The promotion party was celebrated in style at Stark's Park on Saturday 9th April with a 3-1 return over Raith Rovers with the Saints goals coming from Frank McGarvey, John Mowat and Derek Hyslop.

However, just like the young waif in 'Oliver', the Paisley faithful were asking for more!

The fans were happy having achieved promotion, but they wanted the First Division title and nothing less would appease the young and ambitious manager Ferguson.

Both Dundee and Clydebank were the out-in-front contenders to accompany St Mirren upstairs and the crunch came with Saints visiting the City of Discovery to take on Dundee in the penultimate match of the campaign on Tuesday 19th April.

The pre-match buzz surrounded a possible defensive problem for St Mirren.

Jack Copland was in trouble with a suspected cartilage problem and had a consultation with a specialist. He might have played, but Ferguson didn't want to aggravate the injury and thus Copland was rested for the clash at Dens Park.

Bobby Reid was the replacement and his fitness was equally in doubt.

He had played in the last home match with Airdrie three days earlier and was substituted as a precaution after scoring the opening goal in the 3-0 win.

If you want to register your title as First Division champions, you want to achieve the accolade with some style and St Mirren certainly rose to the occasion with a magnificent turnover of Dundee on their home patch.

This young St Mirren side stood on the threshold of greatness.

The 4,000 fans who watched these exciting young players destroy Dundee were privileged to have a vision of the Paisley team's bright future.

This confident Saints side travelled to Dens Park

expecting to harvest two points and, thanks to the brilliance of hat trick hero Frank McGarvey, the citizens of Paisley were able to celebrate a famous win.

St Mirren chairman Willie Todd, a life long supporter, declared it was the finest St Mirren performance in the last 50 years.

Ferguson was equally fulsome. He said, 'The team deserved all the praise. I don't think the winning of this championship is the maximum they can achieve.'

For Tony Fitzpatrick, the leader of this liberated football band, the title meant more to him than playing for his country, although he would love to have emulated both experiences.

As for goal hero McGarvey, this match brought a first for him.

He explained, 'This was the first time I had scored a first class hat trick, although I had done it for the Reserves but the occasion of this match was the time to do it.'

John Young was magnificent in defence and when referee Rollo Kyle blew for time up, he led the players over to the 2,000 travelling St Mirren fans who responded by bedecking their heroes with garlands in black and white.

The euphoria all started in the 39th minute when Billy Stark, back in superb scoring form, scored with a low drive after keeper Ally Donaldson had punched clear from a corner.

A minute later McGarvey sent Saints further along the title trail in taking a measured pass from Stark to bury a tremendous shot beyond the stranded Dundee keeper.

These goals gave St Mirren a 2-0 interval lead and all the confidence to go on and finish the job.

There were 67 minutes on the clock when McGarvey was again on hand to pick up a great pass from Peter Leonard to fire in Saints third.

Leonard, who came on as a substitute for Robert Torrance, laid on yet another pass for the McGarvey hat trick in sweeping home a goal executed with supreme quality.

Final score 4-0, the title in the bag with an unscheduled stop on the way home by the team bus at a Dundee hostelry for further 'light refreshments.' Ah, the sweet wine of success.

Postscript: It was Clydebank who accompanied St Mirren back to Division One, they finished on the 58 point mark - four behind Saints and seven ahead of Dundee.

Teams:

Dundee: *Donaldson, Gemmell, Johnston, Ford, Philip, McPhail, Strachan, Robertson, Pirie, Hutchison and Caldwell. Substitutes: Morris and Laing.*

St Mirren: *Hunter, Beckett, Mowat, Fitzpatrick, Reid, Young, Torrance, Stark, McGarvey, Richardson and Hyslop. Substitutes: Leonard and Johnston.*

Referee: *R. Kyle (Glasgow).*

Attendance: 4,386.

Bobby Reid

ST MIRREN 1 LIVERPOOL 1
(LIVERPOOL WIN 5-4 ON PENS)

Centenary Celebration Match

12th December 1977

OME on, it's a time for celebration. It's your birthday and with your birth certificate date stamped as being the 6th of October 1877 you are celebrating your CENTENARY and as such a rather special present is required.

Such is the history of St Mirren Football Club who, along with Celtic, Dumbarton, Heart of Midlothian and Rangers, are the sole survivors of the inaugural Scottish League in 1890-91.

As so often happens, receipt of that special present can be somewhat wayward from the actual birthday and so it was with St Mirren when manager Alex Ferguson and the board were delighted to announce that Liverpool had accepted the invitation to perform for the centenary birthday bash at St Mirren Park on December 12th 1977.

This was indeed a coup for the Saints.

Liverpool were the current holders of the European Cup having disposed of Borussia Monchengladbach by a 3-1 margin in Rome in the 76-77 campaign.

In that season they were still in the European mood having just blitzed SV Hamburg 6-0 in winning the European Super Cup.

St Mirren's pre-match preparations were much more low key.

Early Scottish games in December '77 were in weather danger due to snow and severe frost.

But Ferguson was philosophical about the weather conditions, 'It doesn't matter, as long as the referee can see the lines and the playing surfaces are flat.'

These parameters were put to the test up at Firhill but the wintry conditions prevailed and the December Saints v. Partick Thistle game was off.

So much for the Love Street preparation in advance of the Anglo-Scottish Cup Final.

St Mirren were then heading for Ashton Gate to take on Bristol City facing up to the need to beat 'The Robins' by two clear goals to take the trophy, having lost 2-1 at Love Street.

In effect, it was a black and white disappointment, the 1-1 draw wasn't enough with St Mirren then travelling to Pittodrie to sharpen up their act prior to the arrival of the men from Merseyside.

It wasn't much better in the Granite City, losing 3-1 with Derek Hyslop the only Saint on the score sheet.

Come the centenary match Liverpool, the crowned kings of Europe, had difficulty in quelling a rebellion of their footballing subjects in Paisley where St Mirren were not prepared to be subservient to the masters of the European game.

The Anfield side, an often-imperious outfit, only managed to overcome the battling Buddies after an astonishing climax at Love Street.

After Kenny Dalglish had given the English First Division side the lead in the 51st minute Liverpool held the upper hand.

The Anfield play was cool and assured. They played with a swagger and a confidence born on the back of winning many battles on foreign fields.

Never really extending themselves, Liverpool were made to fight desperately hard by a young St Mirren side whose character and courage was never in question.

What was in doubt was their resourcefulness to wrest the dominance away from the Merseyside masters.

St Mirren achieved that aspect in the 87th minute with a dramatic equaliser from Billy Abercromby, which fuelled the expectations of the 19,000 crowd as they licked their lips at the prospect of a penalty shoot out.

The first eight penalty kicks were despatched with due aplomb. Iain Munro, Derek Hyslop, Alex Beckett and Abercromby doing the needful for St Mirren with Phil Neal, Emlyn Hughes, Terry McDermott and Ray Kennedy replying for the Reds.

Then came high drama.

Frank McGarvey saw keeper Ray Clemence turn his shot over the bar but the spot kick tally remained at 4-4 when Ally Hunter brilliantly saved Jimmy Case's kick.

To the dismay of the Paisley faithful Clemence brought off a superb save to thwart Bobby Reid's penalty.

It was left to David Johnson to score the decider and take the £500 silver salver back to the Liverpool trophy room.

St Mirren learned a lot from the game and must have been impressed with the discipline and strategy of this Liverpool side in which Kennedy was outstanding as he sprayed passes around left, right and centre.

The swift and subtle movement of the ball was another learning factor for the Paisley players, but they themselves were not lacking in imagination.

Inspired by midfield general, Tony Fitzpatrick, Saints had the opportunity to derail the Liverpool bandwagon but their finishing lacked zest.

In the first half Kenny Dalglish had a goal disallowed just as the game was bursting into life.

Two minutes later McGarvey blasted a drive off the post

followed by a fierce drive from Alex Beckett.

Saints keeper Hunter also played his part and his save from a Kennedy piledriver was worth the admission money on its own.

As the game progressed Liverpool looked safe - then came that Abercromby equaliser.

Teams:

St Mirren: *Hunter, Young, Beckett, Fitzpatrick, Reid, Copland, Hyslop, Stark, McGarvey, Abercromby and Munro. Substitutes: Richardson and Leonard.*

Liverpool: *Clemence, Neal, Hughes, Thomson, Hansen, Kennedy, Dalglish, Case, Fairclough, McDermott and Callaghan. Substitutes: Johnson and Thompson.*

Referee: *Ian Foote.*

Attendance: *19,000.*

Doug Somner

ST MIRREN 3   BRISTOL CITY 1

Anglo Scottish Cup Final - 2nd Leg

16th April 1980.

NCE upon a time there was the Texaco Cup.
This competition involved clubs from the UK and the Republic of Ireland who had not qualified for European competition. Inaugurated in 1970-71, the tournament ran for five seasons with any success by Scottish clubs being generously limited.

Both Hearts and Airdrieonians did reach separate finals but respectively lost out to Wolverhampton Wanderers and Derby County.

Sponsored by the American petroleum giant Texaco, the cup lost its appeal as the competition was dominated by English sides. It led to an imbalance of English fixtures which spectators found unattractive and stayed away.

As a result Texaco withdrew its sponsorship with the Phoenix of the Anglo Scottish Cup arising from the petroleum company's ashes to resume a similar competition in 1975-76. This new tourney lasted for a six-year period with St Mirren reaching the final on two occasions.

All games were played on a home and away two legged basis and in 1977-78 St Mirren's first final appearance saw the Buddies face Bristol City. However, they failed to lift the silverware losing 2-1 at Ashton Gate and only drawing 1-1 at Love Street.

Would the 1979-80 campaign be any more successful? Saints had ousted Hibernian by a 4-3 margin in the first round, going on to eliminate Bolton Wanderers 5-4 in the next.

Into the semi-final and a joust with Sheffield United saw the Blades and Saints draw 0-0 at the Bramall Lane Ground.

In the return match, at Love Street, St Mirren recorded a comprehensive 4-0 win the goals coming from Billy Stark, Iain Munro and a double from Doug Somner.

With some irony the final produced another St Mirren and Bristol City confrontation. Would the tables be turned in 1980 and this evolve into a revenge match?

Certainly the pendulum swung St Mirren's way in the first leg at Ashton Gate with Saints taking a two-goal lead into the return leg all thanks to a double from Stark.

What was interesting in this first leg was the appearance in the City line up of one Anthony Charles Fitzpatrick.

Fitzpatrick had been transferred to Bristol City early in the season on the back of a £250,000 deal, but how would he feel in returning to Love Street for the second leg? Would the Saints fans be kind to him?

In fact, Fitzpatrick didn't play.

Had he taken cold feet? The answer was a simple no as Tony explained, 'This final was coming near the end of the season and Bristol City had arranged a close season tour.

'The tour required that all the players had to have a number of vaccinations and my jabs laid me low for a while.

'I would have loved to have played and then maybe party with the St Mirren lads at the end'.

St Mirren went into the final having beaten Kilmarnock

3-1 the previous Saturday - giving them a three point margin in the race with Morton for a UEFA Cup place.

Only 6,700 fans turned up but would the Saints faithful top that figure at the final?

This Bristol City tie was the eighth Saints had played in the various Anglo Scottish games, a win here would give them a five out of eight rating.

The pre-match hype was helped with the announcement that the BBC would broadcast a live commentary on radio.

Manager Jim Clunie was pretty laid back about the whole proceedings.

He said, 'The Anglo Scottish Cup is slightly different to other competitions, like the Renfrewshire Cup, simply because we are playing against English teams.

'And having come out on top of the pile it is always a pleasure to beat an English team.'

The fans, however, reacted and 13,000 turned out to witness a game, which heralded the first ever, Anglo Scottish Cup win by a Scottish side.

In truth, the game was won at Ashton Gate with this match at Love Street in reality being a sideshow.

The first half was semi anti climax with St Mirren taking the field minus Lex Richardson and Alex Beckett.

Goal-less in the first period with words of 'gentle persuasion' being uttered by manager Clunie at the break in such a manner that pleasing both him and the home fans was now a second half must.

Doug Somner responded and made the break through in the 49th minute netting from close range. With the 2-0 scoreline at Ashton Gate and now three goals to the good, it was time to check if the silverware polish was readily available.

The elusive Peter Weir continued to electrify the crowd with his power, speed and close control and with the creative play of Iain Munro in midfield, St Mirren pushed the English side remorselessly on to their back foot.

Somner ensured the trophy was Paisley bound with a second goal in the 69th minute with teenage striker Alan

Logan crafting the icing on the cake with a third 16 minutes from time.

Bristol City did manage a late consolation goal but by then it was too little too late.

Without five regulars, including Tony Fitzpatrick, the English side's gesture to pull back the deficit was completely lacking in commitment and drive.

It was questionable as to whether or not Bristol City justified a place in the competition.

Their passport to the tournament was based on reaching the 13th rung of the English First Division ladder in 1978-79. The word 'plummet' then enters the English club's dictionary.

Being relegated to the Second Division in 1979-80, was followed by a further drop down to the Third Division the next year, only to hit rock bottom with entry into the Fourth Division in 1981-82. Three successive relegation seasons - no wonder Fitzpatrick was glad to escape back to Love Street in time for the 1981-82 campaign.

It was the black eye patched Lord Westwood, the President of the English League, who presented the cup to skipper Jimmy Bone to be carried off on the celebratory shoulders of Mark Fulton and Jack Copland.

Teams:

St Mirren: *Thomson, Young, Fulton, Copland, Abercromby, Stark, Munro, Bone, Somner, Logan and Weir. Substitutes : Money and Curran.*

Bristol City: *Shaw, Sweeney, Mabbutt, Jantunen, Tainton, Mann, Hay, Gillies, Doyle, Stevens and Baddeley. Substitute : Smith.*

Attendance: *13,000.*

Jim Clunie

ELFSBORG 1   ST MIRREN 2

UEFA Cup 1st Round 1st Leg

17th September 1980

HINK final league placements in the top Scottish Division. Think St Mirren Football Club.

And, in trawling the league records, one would find that the Buddies best ever league finish occurred way back in season 1892-93 when they finished in the traditional bronze medal position just behind Rangers and Celtic, although they did draw home and away with the Ibrox club.

So what were the financial riches for such a placement? Not a lot, with the annual Report Card probably being endorsed with a 'Working to capacity, must do better'. Fast forward to season 1979-80 when Aberdeen won the Premier Division by one point from Celtic, with St Mirren happy to cling onto the third rung of the league ladder.

So, 87 years on and the rewards were considerable with qualification into the UEFA Cup competition.

The 1st Round tie saw Saints drawn to play Elfsborg over in Boras in Sweden.

At the time of the match, Elfsborg were placed fifth in the Swedish First Division whereas St Mirren, eighth in the 10-team Premier League, had just lost 1-0 to Partick Thistle, at Firhill, on the preceding Saturday.

St Mirren had a bit of a Scandinavian taster during the previous week.

Teenage striker Alan Logan was over in Sweden for an Under-21 match with the Scandinavians at Degerfors with the redoubtable Jock Stein in charge as team manager.

The Swedes had a bit of a pre-match problem. The recognised UEFA approved ball was not available in Sweden with an SOS being sent by Elfsborg to Love Street - 'Send us an approved ball so our keeper can get the feel of it.'

What was never recorded was who took the ball over.

The Love Street party left Paisley on the Tuesday with considerable heart searching for Mark Fulton.

Long before the UEFA fixtures had been arranged Fulton and his fiancee, Linda, had made all the arrangements for their wedding. The date so chosen was the Monday before flying out to Sweden with the couple having to endure an extremely restricted honeymoon.

The Buddies were made to feel welcome, not only by their hosts, but also by the typical Paisley inclement weather.

Rain drenched the players constantly throughout the hectic 90 minutes.

The Saints spirits, however, were lifted by a pipe band and the noisy backing of the 200 travelling Love Street fans who had each forked out £3.60 in admission tickets.

The Love Street side went behind to an early goal from Swedish Under-21 striker Lenart Nilsson and struggled to subdue the home outfit.

St Mirren had made it difficult for themselves with only 15 minutes played.

A defensive mix up between Jackie Copland and keeper Billy Thomson let in Nilsson to net from close range.

The St Mirren heads weren't in any way down, nor their confidence in any way diminished.

It showed just a couple of minutes from the interval break with a Route One orientated goal.

A long ball from John McCormack helped demonstrate the prolific marksmanship powers of Doug Somner who neatly turned the ball past keeper Roger Svensson for the equaliser.

Never a bad time to net an equaliser and, when St Mirren returned after the break, one could visibly see the spirit - 'We can win this game.'

Manager Jim Clunie had had some European experience in his time with Southampton.

Alex Ferguson was a close buddie of Clunie's and his proffered advice was simple - 'Great patience will be required.'

That patience factor soon signalled the rise of St Mirren's attacking flair and the decline of Elfsborg, whose spirit was no match for the Scots superiority in strength and skill.

However, with the margin so tight the Swedes were always going to be a threat until Billy Abercromby volleyed home a pass from Billy Stark for the winner in the 70th minute.

St Mirren could have recorded a more decisive return, but the Finnish referee disallowed a Frank McDougall effort, apparently for offside, with the score tied at 1-1.

The home team made two second half substitutions to try and turn the game their way, but St Mirren were not to be denied and were clearly the better team on the day.

Clunie was a delighted manager who had hoped for a clear-cut victory, plus, having scored two away goals, confidence was high for the return leg at Love Street in a fortnight's time.

Saints were under considerable criticism at home for a string of inconsistent displays, but they thrived on their European debut with Copland, Peter Weir and Lex Richardson the prime players with their skill and ingenuity.

Postscript: Two weeks later, on 1st October with a less-than-convincing display, St Mirren qualified for the 2nd Round on the back of a 0-0 draw with Elfsborg at Love Street.

Teams:

Elfsborg: *R. Svensson, Qvist, L Johansson, Ahlstrom, Malberg, Klarstrom, I Svensson, Nilsson, Gustafsson, T Johansson and Anderson. Substitute: Gustawson, Hansson, Heliqvist and Stenbacken.*

St Mirren: *Thomson, Young, Beckett, Richardson, McCormack, Copland, Abercromby, Stark, Somner, Weir and McDougall. Substitute: Fulton and Logan.*

Attendance: *3,800.*

Alex Beckett

CELTIC 1 ST MIRREN 2

Premier League

22nd November 1980

 VISIT to Celtic Park might well be anticipated with some trepidation.

Leaving the east end of Glasgow with a full complement of league points is not a ready pastime for the lads from Love Street.

Having said that, home in on the results between the sides in the 1977-78 season when both Parkhead fixtures ended in 2-1 wins for the Buddies as the St Mirren strike force had such luminaries as Billy Stark, Frank McGarvey and Derek Hyslop.

Generally, you can generate a fair package of excitement into a 90-minute tussle, but in this latest confrontation with the Parkhead Hoops the game only climaxed in the last few minutes.

It was St Mirren right back Alex Beckett who sent Celtic sprawling to their third successive home defeat with his first goal of the season and arguably, the most spectacular of his career.

It came when the frustrated Celtic fans had gratefully settled for a draw after George McCluskey had equalised from the penalty spot in the 85th minute.

Smarting from referee Mike Delaney in giving a penalty when Tommy Burns went down without an apparent tackle on him, St Mirren buzzed angrily around the Celtic goal in the closing minutes.

With two minutes to go they forced a corner on the right to be taken by their most industrious player Peter Weir. The big fellow lobbed an in-swinger into the crowded box where Tom McAdam cleanly headed clear.

As the ball dropped some 25 yards from the goal line Beckett took it on the drop and smashed the ball with incredible power high into the Celtic net. Poor Pat Bonner hadn't an earthly - he just didn't see it!

What a winner and what a climax to a game that was more sour than sweet, although the last five minutes certainly improved the sugar content of the occasion.

Celtic were frantic in their desperation to avoid their fourth home defeat in a row.

Indeed, St Mirren were more creative in fashioning scoring opportunities and might have opened the scoring in just the fourth minute when a loose pass from McAdam put Doug Somner in the clear. For some reason Somner passed the chance to Jimmy Bone who immediately returned the pass and the chance was lost.

Celtic's only opportunity in the first half came when Burns sidled in between Beckett and Jack Copland to whip a right foot drive over the St Mirren crossbar.

Roddie MacDonald was booked for a foul on Somner in this half and in the second period Abercromby, Willie Fulton and the Celtic skipper Danny McGrain were all introduced to referee Delaney's wee black note book for fairly innocuous offences.

McAdam saved the Celtic goal in the 55th minute when he jumped to clear a Stark lob from just under the bar when it had totally beaten Bonner.

It began to look as if a no scoring draw was on the cards.

However, six minutes from the final whistle the game ignited into some real action.

A Weir cross from the left wasn't cleared properly and, as the ball bobbled around the Celtic goal area, the human dynamo that is Lex Richardson burst through to smash it low into the net.

A minute later down went Burns just inside the box in what is now termed vintage simulation as the Saints defence covered desperately, but match official Delaney, had no mercy and presented Celtic with that penalty.

The entire St Mirren team protested vehemently but the man in black from Cleland pointed to the spot and refused to consult his linesmen.

McCluskey, who had replaced Charlie Nicholas at half time, hammered the ball home.

It looked for all the world like a pools punter's dream with the possible draw until Beckett sealed his St Mirren immortality with that cracking goal.

Teams:

Celtic: *Bonner, McGrain, MacDonald, McAdam, Reid, Sullivan, Aitken, Weir, Burns, Nicholas (McCluskey) and McGarvey. Substitute not used: Doyle.*

St Mirren: *Thomson, Beckett, Fulton, Copland, Abercromby, Richardson, McCormack, Weir, Stark, Bone and Somner. Substitutes not used: McDougall and Young.*

Referee: *Mike Delaney (Cleland).*

Attendance: *16,000.*

Jimmy Bone

ST MIRREN 1 ABERDEEN 1

Premier League

3rd January 1981

HAT constitutes a 'classic match' I hear you ask? Generally such a game hits the archives when Saints do the needful and harvest the full complement of league points on offer, or can post a cup tie win.

Occasionally, a draw can catch the classic headlines and this January confrontation with Aberdeen more than fits the bill.

The build up to this game was intriguing.

St Mirren had lost their opening game of the season to the Dons on the back of a 0-1 scoreline at Love Street.

Saints had also lost 3-2 up at Pittodrie, but their appetite for this third league game was spiced up with the Buddies New Year's Day derby with Morton. The 3-1 win at Cappielow being more than acceptable to the substantial travelling Paisley support.

Aberdeen had just won the top league title for only the

second time in their history, the 1979-80 campaign being the first under the tutelage of the former St Mirren manager Alex Ferguson.

Everything was going swimmingly for the Granite City side, cue the performance of one Bridge of Allan born James Bone - now in his third spell with the Saints having rejoined them from the Toronto Blizzards side in Canada.

It was Bone who left his mark on the game with a goal in the 54th minute.

And, it was a goal of classic proportions, which must have been a serious contender for Goal of the Season if not of the Decade.

It proved once and for all that there's life in the 'old dog' that was Bone Esquire although Jimmy would be more than happy to point out that he had only blown out 31 candles on his last birthday cake.

The goal-scoring move started with a pass from John Young to Peter Weir who simply helped it on its way to Bone on the half way line.

Off went the bold Bone as if the seat of his pants were on fire. He slalomed his way through the Aberdeen defence leaving four Pittodrie defenders trailing in his slipstream.

On and on went Bone and as keeper Jim Leighton confronted him just inside the box, he neatly poked the ball under him and into the net - terrific!

It was then the turn of former Saints winger Ian Scanlon to pull the Dons back from the brink for the second time in a week.

He did it from the penalty spot against Dundee United on the Tuesday and came up with a repeat to thwart his former team mates in a fiery encounter.

Still St Mirren were now unbeaten in their last six matches nestling nicely on the sixth rung of the 10-team league ladder with Aberdeen leading the pack.

It was a clash of more fire than finesse and as a spectacle was almost ruined by a gale force wind.

In fact, when Aberdeen failed to take any advantage of the breeze in the first half they seemed to be heading for big trouble as St Mirren powered in on Leighton.

Aberdeen though had different ideas and, driven on by the inexhaustible Andy Watson, they kept their cool and worked their way towards Billy Thomson.

They got a lucky breakthrough in the 68th minute when Neil Simpson, running into the box, was floored by John McCormack.

Everyone with a black and white affinity was convinced the challenge was fair and above board.

Referee McGunnigle had no second thoughts - penalty and Scanlon was equally positive in launching the spot kick high into the net.

This was the fourth consecutive match in which the Dons have been awarded a penalty. With the execution of the goals there were few other clear-cut chances.

Biggest let off for Saints came from Mark McGhee.

Put through by Simpson, his first drive was brilliantly parried by keeper Billy Thomson with the rebound being thundered off the upright.

In the main, the defences came out on top with both teams being well marshalled by their respective skippers Jackie Copland and Willie Miller.

In these days, when heartburn is a fact of life, one is inclined to feel one's age - Jimmy Bone doesn't as he was here, there and everywhere and was rightly crowned Man of the Match.

Teams:

St Mirren: *Thomson, Young, Copland, Fulton, Beckett, Stark, Richardson, McCormack, Bone, Somner and Weir. Substitutes not used: McDowall and Abercromby.*

Aberdeen: *Leighton, Kennedy, McLeish, Miller, Rougvie, Simpson, Watson, Angus, McCall (Hewitt), McGhee and Scanlon. Substitute not used: Jarvie.*

Referee: *A McGunnigle (Glasgow).*

Estimated Attendance: *11,100.*

Billy Stark

AIRDRIEONIANS 3   ST MIRREN 4

Scottish Premier League

5th September 1981

THE start of the 1981-82 season saw the League Cup campaign revert from the straight knock out format to the original sectionalised pattern.

St Mirren had drawn St Johnstone, Hibernian and Celtic in their group with much jubilation when Saints topped the section by a single point.

To win 3-1 at Celtic Park was always a morale booster, but the Love Street feathers were more than slightly ruffled when the Parkhead side recorded a 5-1 win in the return fixture.

What was significant was the debut of a new hero in Ian Scanlon who had arrived from Aberdeen in part exchange with Peter Weir who had moved to Pittodrie courtesy of a £220,000 transfer fee.

Scanlon made his debut in the League Cup competition and really made the Saints fans sit up when the bearded winger scored both goals against St Johnstone at Love

Street to secure St Mirren's quarter final placement against Forfar Athletic.

But that double wasn't enough for Scanlon.

The first Premier League match of the season saw Saints at home to perennial Renfrewshire rivals Morton and Mr Scanlon went on to seal his love affair with the Saints fans with another double.

His first goal came from the penalty spot with the second being reminiscent of a 20 yard guided missile as it exploded behind keeper Roy Baines.

A dramatic start to the season, but the real drama was to unfold in Saints' second game against Airdrieonians at their Broomfield ground.

St Mirren gave a full first team start to one Frank McAvennie.

McAvennie had logged in a substitute's appearance against Partick Thistle in the previous league season and had been on the bench for the aforementioned Morton game.

However, this Airdrie game was the stage to establish McAvennie as a cult figure with the Saints fans as the youngster went on to score two sensational goals to give his side an unbelievable football feast.

There was no scoring in the first half and the first indication of an unpredictable afternoon came soon after the interval when Saints shocked Airdrie with two goals right out of the blue.

In the 61st minute McAvennie went on a mazy, solo run by taking on the entire Airdrie defence to push a simple ball out of keeper John Martin's reach.

The quality of the cheeky strike was breathtaking as it heralded the first McAvennie strike in the senior game.

Three minutes later it seemed to be all over when Billy Stark netted from a Scanlon corner. Saints were cruising - but only for a minute.

An immediate retaliation from the Diamonds saw Sandy Clark scoring from the penalty spot after referee Jim Renton had adjudged Frank McDougall had impeded Jim Rodger in the box.

Saints were taken further aback before they had any time to recover when Tommy Walker headed home a cross from John Flood for the equaliser in the 66th minute.

If that wasn't bad enough for St Mirren, worse was to follow. With 71 minutes on the clock, Airdrie turned the tables upside down again when they took the lead through Clark in taking a pass from Tommy Walker to beat Billy Thomson all ends up.

Two minutes to go and Saints were getting desperate. Many of the fans shared the team's desperation with considerable numbers heading for the exits to bemoan the anticipated result on a sorry full journey back to Paisley.

Enter Stark to provide the equaliser when he bulleted a ferocious drive past the luckless Martin in the 88th minute.

The sounds of triumphal relief reverberated around the Paisley fans. Those that heard the commotion and were half way down the terracing stairs stopped and returned for the finale causing some considerable health and safety problems with the melee.

Saints were now level, what chance the possibility of a winner? One minute to go and the debut boy McAvennie did the business when he pounced on a loose ball to slam home the winner to send the Love Street fans wild.

Manager Rikki McFarlane would be a happy laddie with this performance. St Mirren, after only two games, were level with Celtic at the top of the Premier League - bring on the world!

They did bring on Rangers for the next game which ended in a 1-1 draw, but that is another story.

Teams:

Airdrieonians: *Martin, Erwin, March, McCluskey, Rodger, Walker, Gordon, McGuire, McKeown, Clark and Flood. Substitutes unused: Thompson and Campbell.*

St Mirren: *Thomson, Beckett, McCormack, Copland, Abercromby, Richardson, Stark, Scanlon, Logan (McDougall), Bone and McAvennie. Substitute unused: Young.*

Referee: *Mr Jim Renton, Cowdenbeath.*

Attendance: *3,500.*

Billy Thomson

ST MIRREN 4 MORTON 3

Scottish Cup 5h Round

10th March 1984

T MIRREN had managed to collect a couple of byes in the first two rounds of the 1983-84 Scottish Cup competition.

In the 2nd Round the Buddies were drawn to face Meadowbank Thistle within the vast acres of the Meadowbank Stadium in Edinburgh.

It wasn't a match to set the pulses racing and to be honest most 0-0 scorelines never do. Would the replay at Love Street be any better?

Certainly there were goals here with a double from Neil Cooper - wearing the No 4 shirt - contributing to the Buddies earning yet another draw - 2-2 this time.

For the deciding replay a coin was tossed to determine the choice of venue with St Mirren having to journey back along the M8 to face Meadowbank again on their home patch.

Goals from Frank McAvennie and Ian Scanlon in a 2-1

win saw St Mirren drawn to play Hamilton Accies in the 4th Round at Love Street. Another 2-1 result materialised thanks to the St Mirren goal scoring efforts of Willie Fulton and Frank McDougall.

Into the 5th Round, with whoops of anticipation being loudly heard across the county, when Morton followed St Mirren out of the crystal bowl.

The imagination of a tasty tie was now to be further spiced with the old Renfrewshire rivals being paired at Love Street.

Morton manager Tommy McLean had a major problem.

He tried to have the cup tie postponed due to a catalogue of injuries and illness. However, the SFA came down heavily with a Park Gardens directive - 'As long as you have 13 fit players the tie goes ahead.'

In truth, the pattern of this Renfrewshire derby was portrayed before the game had even started.

Having led his heroes on to the park, St Mirren's young mascot wobbled, slipped and measured his length twice on his return journey to the touchline, the first mistakes of an error ridden afternoon, but never the less entertaining one.

The overall assessment of the game could be headlined as the tale of two penalties - one a penalty of fame the other a penalty of infamy.

Both goalkeepers gave away spot kicks at vital moments.

The difference was that the Buddies keeper, Billy Thomson, wasn't punished for his error whereas Murray McDermott was.

Penalty No 1 came as Morton were leading 2-1 and moving well.

Thomson came charging out in the 35th minute and clattered Dom Sullivan into the turf.

Sullivan opted to take the kick himself ... and smashed the ball against the right hand post before it ran wide.

Penalty No 2 arrived in the 71st minute when the score was 2-2.

McDermott came out and flapped at a cross and in so doing clattered McDougall in the back.

This time Ian Scanlon netted the kick in his usual accomplished manner.

And just to ensure St Mirren's passage to the semi finals for the third year in a row, Scanlon pounced to make it 4-2 three minutes later.

A goal from that arch-scoring predator Willie Pettigrew came too late for Morton and even from the diehards of the St Mirren following, few would argue that the Cappielow side deserved at least a replay.

Saints had opened the scoring when McAvennie ripped through the left flank of the Morton defence in the sixth minute to beat McDermott with a fierce drive.

But ex-Ranger Dougie Robertson - a constant thorn in the Love Street rearguard - neatly headed the equaliser in the 17th minute.

And on the half hour another scoring Robertson header had St Mirren rocking with the thought that the Buddies might have toppled if that penalty had gone in.

It was Tony Fitzpatrick who brought parity to the proceedings when he netted the equaliser just a minute before half time with a well-taken drive.

Postscript: St Mirren went on to play Celtic in the semi finals at Hampden, but lost 2-1.

Teams:

St Mirren: *Thomson, Jarvie, Clarke, Cooper, Fulton, McCormack, Fitzpatrick, McAvennie, McDougall (Alexander), Abercromby and Scanlon.*

Morton: *McDermott, Houston, Holmes, Duffy, Welsh (Turner), Sullivan, Robertson, Docherty, Pettigrew, Rooney and Doak.*

Referee: *Hugh Alexander (Kilmarnock).*

Attendance: *7,933.*

Gardner Speirs

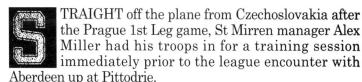

ST MIRREN 3 SLAVIA PRAGUE 0

UEFA Cup 1st Round 2nd Leg
2nd October 1985

STRAIGHT off the plane from Czechoslovakia after the Prague 1st Leg game, St Mirren manager Alex Miller had his troops in for a training session immediately prior to the league encounter with Aberdeen up at Pittodrie.

A legacy from playing behind that iron curtain was the steely resolve in evidence at the Granite City game.

The match finished 1-1 with both goals coming from the penalty spot with Gardner Speirs on target for Saints.

In between the two UEFA ties, the promise for Saints in the future was demonstrated by Norrie McWhirter and Paul Lambert, bosom Buddies both on and off the

pitch, as they made their international debuts for the national Under-16 side winning 2-1 against Iceland in Reykjavik.

The pre-Slavia return tie was a scheduled league fixture with Dundee United at Love Street and would provide an incentive for Saints in that a win would see them two points above the Tannadice men.

Another game, another win, and another Speirs penalty with league daylight now clear between the Arabs and the Buddies.

As a means of UEFA belief and build up, it was mission accomplished even though the winning goal was a last minute conversion.

Prices for the return leg were very much in line with those at St Mirren's last Euro tie with the Dutch giants Feyenoord two seasons ago.

Tickets went on sale at the St Mirren Shop in the Piazza. Admission to the stand was £5 with season tickets not valid for the game.

However, the board partially relented and decided that season ticket holders may purchase their own seat at a discounted price of £4.

It was a cash admission at all other parts of the ground with the enclosure rated at £3 with concessions at £2.50 and the terracing priced at £2.50 and £1.50.

Assistant manager Martin Ferguson had undertaken an in-depth analysis of the Prague players and was at length to point out that Slavia would field almost half the Czech national side.

In particular for the St Mirren strike force the two central defenders both had outstanding talents.

The result was a personal triumph for the battle-scarred Frank McGarvey who won his personal war of attrition to take St Mirren into the next round of the UEFA Cup.

The resilient Paisley striker twice breached Slavia Prague's iron curtain defence in extra time ensuring a Paisley representation in the draw in Zurich.

The weakness of the Norwegian referee, Rolf Haugen,

gave the Slavia defenders a legacy to kick McGarvey all over the Love Street pitch ensuring the Saints front man would be sporting a selection of black and blue bruises in the morning.

However, McGarvey, dubbed the rubber man by the Paisley faithful, had the last laugh with two overtime match winning strikes.

He instantly became the local hero with his will-to-win performance, which was mirrored by his team mates, and, not surprisingly, he collected a well-deserved Man of the Match award.

Although there was a certain element of luck with the first two goals from Brian Gallagher and McGarvey, Saints always looked the more likely to score despite their early play bordering on being over frantic and naive.

Yet when the first goal arrived in the 42nd minute it was no more than deserved. Gallagher saw his shot deflected home after keeper Hruska had parried a Speirs effort.

St Mirren, who had to replace the injured Steve Clarke with Ian Scanlon in the 74th minute, fought fiercely for that second goal, but Slavia, who had Kubic, Janu, Jarolim and Sokol all booked, grew stronger as the game progressed.

Despite all the intense Paisley pressure the goal remained elusive after the allotted 90 minutes.

Step forward that man McGarvey and, with 11 minutes of the first period of extra time on the clock, he drove in a shot, which was defected, into the net by Jeslinek.

However, there was nothing fortuitous about the clinching third goal. McGarvey, still tormenting the tiring Czech defenders, brilliantly flicked a pass from substitute Kenny McDowall into the net to give the Paisley patrons a full licence to celebrate into the 'wee sma' hours.'

With Celtic out of the European Cup Winners' Cup competition thanks to a turnover from Atletico Madrid at Parkhead and Rangers' elimination from the UEFA Cup all due to Osasuna, another Spanish club, it left St Mirren as the sole west of Scotland club remaining in European contention.

Teams:

St Mirren: *Money, Wilson, Hamilton, Rooney, Godfrey, Clarke, Fitzpatrick, Cooper, McGarvey, Gallagher and Speirs. Substitutes: Scanlon and McDowall.*

Slavia Prague: *Hruska, Sokol, Kubic, Takac, Jeslinek, Jarolim, Nemec, Dolezal, Fryde, Janu and Viger. Substitutes: Konril and Rehac.*

Referee: *Rolf Haugen (Norway).*

Attendance: *11,786*

Brian Gallagher

HAMMARBY IF 3   ST MIRREN 3

UEFA Cup 2nd Round 1st Leg

23rd October 1985

HAIRMAN Yule Craig returned from the UEFA principality in Zurich happy to have drawn Hammarby IF in the UEFA Cup 2nd Round.

He was pleased in having met the Hammarby officials, but most folk back in Paisley were completely in the dark as to the who, the where, the why and when regarding St Mirren's opponents.

Hammarby Fotboll is a Swedish football club based in Sodermalm, the southern most district of the Stockholm city centre.

In Sweden, the club is often referred to by its nickname Bajen - a short form of a mock English pronunciation of 'Hammarby'.

Formed in 1889 as Hammarby Roddforening - effectively Hammarby Rowing Association - in 1897 the name was changed to Hammarby Idrottsforening, as many of the club's athletes were now engaged in a wide variety of sports other than rowing. And 1915 saw the separate establishment of the Hammarby Fotboll side.

The Swedish League is titled the Allsvenskan with Hammarby coming to the fore in the 1980s by virtue of runner-up spots in both their national League and Cups.

Hammarby for many years was classified as a yo-yo club having achieved promotion and relegation on a regular basis.

However, at the time of this UEFA tie with St Mirren they had to be taken seriously, as in the 1st round they had demolished the Bulgarian side Blagoegrad 7-1 on aggregate.

As for Saints, their pre-UEFA warm up match was a league encounter with Dundee at Love Street. Gardner Speirs was becoming pretty adept at pinching league points with penalties and he was at it again - his sole strike being enough to deflate the Dens Park side and consolidate St Mirren's fourth spot in the Premier League ladder.

But the Saints injury count was prodigious.

Tony Fitzpatrick and Derek Hamilton both missed the Dundee game, while Peter Godfrey played the entire game with a broken nose. Further problems surrounded Tommy Wilson who came off with a knee injury to be replaced by Neil Cooper.

There was no doubt that the visiting Hammarby coach Bjorn Boling, who took in the Dundee match, would see a totally different St Mirren team in ten days' time.

It wasn't the build-up one might expect in a match immediately prior to a European tie and Alex Miller let his charges know in no uncertain manner by castigating his team for a most untimely slump in the 3-0 defeat to Hearts at Tynecastle.

Saints flew out to Sweden on the Tuesday prior to the game with manager Miller promising to axe his under-performing players from this Stockholm excursion. The St Mirren line up would be interesting.

One Buddie who was subsequently excused from any criticism was bustling striker Brian Gallagher whose goal scoring exploits left the Paisley Saints just 90 minutes from a place in the 3rd Round.

Gallagher, so often the tireless worker in the shadow of Frank McGarvey, emerged as the hero of St Mirren's superb performance. C'mon now - three away goals and all from one player.

Ill luck, indecision and a controversial penalty combined to give Hammarby a 3-1 decisive lead with only eight minutes to go.

But the Swedes hadn't reckoned with the galloping Gallagher who restored Saints' cup chances with two late goals.

It was all that St Mirren deserved. They won over the admiration of the 4,000 crowd in the Soderstadion with their all-action attacking play.

If Gallagher, cheered on by a small group of friends working over in Sweden, proved the goal scoring inspiration, manager Miller turned out to be the master tactician in guiding his team closer to Euro success.

Miller was confident the return leg at Love Street would now attract between 12,000 and 15,000.

St Mirren playing with maturity and confidence dominated the first half, but went in at the break 2-1 down.

After the superbly efficient McGarvey and Speirs had goals disallowed for offside, St Mirren went surprisingly behind when Thomas Lundin scored from close range in the 32nd minute when a free kick wasn't cleared.

However, Gallagher equalised three minutes from the interval with a well-taken goal.

Then controversy.

Hammarby were awarded a penalty with seconds to go to the break after Neil Cooper had floored the Hammarby frontman.

St Mirren were incensed, insisting that the Swede was offside, but Czech referee Dusa Krchnak waved away the Paisley players protests and Anderson stepped up to restore Hammarby's lead.

St Mirren continued to be the more progressive side, but

in the 65th minute a dreadful mistake by Tommy Wilson in belting the ball against his own cross bar allowed Anderson to cotton on to the loose ball and make it 3-1 to the hosts.

However, St Mirren, with Peter Mackie on for Kenny McDowall, had their saviour in Gallagher when sheer opportunism won him two more goals in the dying minutes to send the travelling Buddies home happy.

Teams:

Hammarby: *Skalleberg, Gronquist, Vaattovaara, Dennerby, Johansson, Turesson, Romberg, Andersson, Wahlberg, Lundin and Eriksson.*

St Mirren: *Money, Wilson, Hamilton, Rooney, Cooper, Clarke, Fitzpatrick, McDowall (Mackie), Gallagher, McGarvey and Speirs.*

Referee: *Mr Dusa Krchnak, (Czechoslovakia)*

Tony Fitzpatrick

ST MIRREN 1   HAMMARBY 2

UEFA Cup 2nd Round 2nd Leg

6th November 1985

I T is to be thankful that the St Mirren fans are a stoical lot blessed with the ability to take joy and misery in copious portions.

Have a look at the scenario immediately prior to the return UEFA crunch game with Hammarby at Love Street.

Only 10 days before the tie and Rangers visit Love Street. A 2-1 win over the Ibrox side, so cue emotions of total joy with Saintly feelings perhaps being deceived into thinking they are a better team than they really are.

Then, four days before the arrival of the Swedes, Saints are on duty at Fir Park.

Now here we have Motherwell languishing at the foot of the table with Saints happily ensconced fourth top in the Premier League. If ever there was an away banker it was here at Fir Park.

Not quite! St Mirren even took the lead against the

Steelmen with a brilliantly headed goal from Peter Godfrey in the 34th minute. Game over thought the Saints and sat back!

No way insisted the Fir Parkers who focused, upped their work rate and their commitment with the speedy John Gahagan going on to net two and Brian Wright converting a penalty.

Only Steve Clarke, St Mirren's Scotland Under-21 defender, emerged with any credit. Although caught out of position on occasion, his general performance was worthy of praise.

The lack of goals was a worry for Alex Miller - particularly when former Saint, Frank McAvennie, now with West Ham, had 14 goals to his credit keeping him top of the English Division One scoring charts.

The immediate pre-match feelings about Hammarby were that if St Mirren could grab an early goal the Swedish side would be running scared.

That much-cherished goal arrived in the 20th minute.

The industrious Tony Fitzpatrick, the only member of a poor midfield to show any spark of life, won a corner. Gardner Speirs' flag kick was headed onto the bar by Godfrey before Frank McGarvey, with cool opportunism, blasted the ball past keeper Skalleberg.

But St Mirren were given an early warning regarding the danger of lack of vigilance.

Keeper Campbell Money kept the Saints goal intact and some weak Paisley finishing kept the score sheet blank, until the home team made that breakthrough with one of their more positive attacks.

It was downhill sadly for Saints after that.

Instead of exerting more pressure to register the decisive second goal, they lost their way.

Their play deteriorated dramatically, although the Swedes failed to cotton on to the fact that St Mirren were there for the taking.

The visitors did little to demonstrate that they were about to orchestrate a shattering and embarrassing result.

St Mirren, particularly in midfield, didn't inject their play after the interval with any venom to inspire their fans.

They allowed Hammarby too much room to manoeuvre and be creative thus confidently raising their prospects of a win.

Hammarby began to believe in themselves and two late substitutions with Thomas Lundin replacing Ohlsson and Ivarsson coming on for Vandenburg brought fresh legs and a greater will to win into their play.

St Mirren still held the balance of power, but were living on borrowed time.

In the 87th minute the substitute Ivarsson drilled home the equaliser with the home defence in total disarray.

Still the score stood at 1-1 and, if the score remained that way, St Mirren would still go through.

It didn't! Hammarby had the ball in the net again but it was disallowed. Seconds later with a minute to go Andersson became an instant Swedish hero when he fired in the winner. Jubilant Swedes - distraught Saints!!

St Mirren had committed the football version of Hara Kari to exit ingloriously from the UEFA Cup at a rain swept Love Street.

Thus Saints denied themselves the opportunity to line up against the top clubs in the next round. The galling inner feeling was that the defeat was all of their own making.

Not one home supporter could have any sympathy for a team who, having scored three European goals away from home and taken the lead in the home leg, threw away the opportunity to make history.

Teams:

St Mirren: *Money, Wilson, Hamilton, Rooney, Godfrey, Clarke, Fitzpatrick, Mackie, McGarvey, Gallagher and Speirs. Substitutes : Abercromby and McDowall.*

Hammarby: *Skalleberg, Vonderburg, Holberg, Vaattovaara, Johanson, Uhlback, Romberg, Andersson, Turesson, Ohlsson and Eriksson. Substitutes: Lundin and Ivarsson.*

Referee: *I.B. Nielson (Denmark).*

Attendance: *12,000.*

Frank McGarvey

ST MIRREN 2   HEART OF MIDLOTHIAN 1

Scottish Cup Semi-Final

11th April 1987

LEARLY the media were hugely disappointed when they found that neither Rangers nor Celtic would be participating at the semi-final stage of the 1987 Scottish Cup competition.

How on earth would they fill their column inches?

Perhaps a modicum of research would have revealed that this match would be St Mirren's 17th Scottish Cup semi-final participation, with four such appearances coming in the last six seasons.

The media flavour certainly had their pennies being deposited in favour of a Hearts v. Dundee final as being the current form teams.

Indeed, the bookies were going to the extremes in offering 1000-1 against a St Mirren v. Dundee United get together at Hampden. We would see if their odds were misplaced!

What was interesting was the other semi featuring

Dundee and Dundee United, a City of Discovery team would certainly be in the final.

It had taken Saints 25 years to go marching into another Scottish Cup final and they did it in a manner full of style and panache.

The Paisley support in the Hampden crowd was considerably outnumbered by their scarf-twirling Edinburgh counterparts, but once the winning goal had gone in then vast acres of open space rapidly appeared in the Tynecastle ranks.

Frank McGarvey, formerly with Saints, Liverpool and Celtic, had now returned to Paisley as the proverbial prodigal son and was now a confirmed Buddie once again.

And once he came up with the goal that counted, then the media's opinion was unanimous - it was a winner well-deserved.

While Hearts revived their chances with a 74th minute goal from Gary Mackay, it was St Mirren who were always the sprightlier and more composed side.

Epitomised by the energetic Ian Ferguson, this reported £60,000 steal from Clyde was the man on track to give St Mirren the lead in the 31st minute.

It was Dave Winnie who created the opening and there was 'Fergie' to beat both keeper Henry Smith and George Cowie, who tried desperately to prevent the ball crossing the line.

While Saints were in an effervescent mood, the Gorgie Road side appeared to be flat and on occasion lifeless, so it was all the more intriguing when they equalised totally against the run of play.

A route one clearance found Cowie way out on the left touchline where he curled in a cross, which Gary Mackay cracked in a shot off the upright.

Eight minutes from the final whistle, Hearts' joy was short-lived when Ian Cameron scampered down the wing to put McGarvey in the clear. He had the merest glimpse of the goal, but the Saints' India rubber man wriggled through to smack the winner past keeper Smith.

Neil Cooper and Winnie earned their spurs in bottling out the Edinburgh strike force while Billy Abercromby, despite receiving another booking, joined with Brian Hamilton and Paul Lambert to sew up the midfield.

Abercromby was joined by Ferguson, who was named Man of the Match, together with John Colquhoun and Kenny McDowall who all found their way into referee Bill Crombie's little black book. He wasn't soliciting Christmas card addresses and all this yellow card mayhem coming from a game that never boiled over.

Hearts were without Walter Kidd, Brian Whittaker and the free scoring John Robertson - all suspended - but that was no excuse for their lacklustre display.

What was disappointing was the size of the crowd which led the pundits to forecast a possible lack of atmosphere at the forthcoming final between Saints and Dundee United.

However, if St Mirren could produce their form, as shown against Hearts and Dundee United, live up to their skilful reputation, then this would be final worth watching.

There will be a larger crowd - the Saints supporters would see to that.

Teams:

St Mirren: *Money, Wilson, Cooper, Winnie, D. Hamilton, B. Hamilton, Lambert (Cameron), Abercromby, Ferguson, McDowall and McGarvey. Substitute not used: McWhirter.*

Hearts:: *Smith, Murray, Jardine, MacDonald, Cowie, Watson (Crabbe), Mackay, Black, Colquhoun, Clarke and Foster. Substitute not used : Sandison.*

Referee: *W.N.M. Crombie.*

Attendance: *32,390.*

Billy Abercromby

ST MIRREN 1 DUNDEE UNITED 0

Scottish Cup Final

16th May 1987

HERE aren't too many in the record books. And 40 years since the end of World War Two hostilities, there have only been seven Scottish Cup finals that didn't feature either Rangers or Celtic.

So, St Mirren v Dundee United would be number eight and clearly emphasised there was more to football than Old Firm rivalries.

Not surprisingly, the Press labelled this match as 'The Peoples Final.'

Saints' progress through the cup tournament had been steady, if not spectacular. A home win in the 3rd Round over Highland League club Inverness Caley preceded away wins over Renfrewshire rivals Morton and then Raith Rovers.

By now both Celtic and Rangers had been eliminated, the latter going down to a shock 1-0 defeat at Ibrox against

Hamilton Accies thanks to a memorable Adrian Sprott goal.

Saints took on Hearts in the semi-final at Hampden while the two Dundee clubs faced each other at Tynecastle in the other tie.

Nerves were largely on show at Hampden before a crowd of 32,390, the game failing to match the occasion with the Paisley plaudits for the 2-1 win going to the goal getting duo of Ian Ferguson and Frank McGarvey.

It was to be hoped that St Mirren would build on this result for their assault on the final but what ensued between semi and final was an uninspiring series of results.

The first Saturday in May saw Saints going down 1-0 to Hamilton, at Douglas Park, to be followed by a 1-0 defeat at Ibrox, with Rangers going on to clinch the Premier Division championship that day, This was not a particularly positive preparation for cup final confidence.

By comparison, Dundee United were going great guns - especially on the UEFA Cup front.

The Tangerines had disposed of Lens, University Craiova, Hadjuk Split, Barcelona, and Borussia Monchengladbach, all quality European sides, before taking on IFK Gothenburg in the two-legged final.

The first leg took place on the Wednesday and, immediately prior to this Scottish Cup final, Saints manager Alex Smith's pre-match preparation included a trip to Sweden to run the rule over United at the Ullevi Stadium.

At Hampden there wasn't much satisfaction in the wake of a no scoring draw, certainly there was plenty of effort and plenty of fans but nothing in the way of goals.

That was the pattern as the 90 minutes ended 0-0 and stuttered into extra time much to the nail-biting nausea of the watching media. Deadlines were going to be tight to meet the Saturday evening sports editions.

For the Terrors from Tannadice this final was the first of a couple of major games in their diaries. They were due to meet IFK Gothenburg in the second leg of the UEFA Cup final on the following Wednesday, so commitment yes, but please no injuries, was the quest.

Major United pressure initially was coming from the towering presence of John Clark. He repeatedly troubled the Saints defence, but full backs Derek Hamilton and Tommy Wilson combined with the agility of Campbell Money kept the eager Dundee front men at bay.

Gradually St Mirren started to make the bookmakers, who had all but written off their chances, look like doubtful judges.

Ian Ferguson and Kenny McDowall went close but former Saints keeper Billy Thomson thwarted both.

Both teams went in at the interval with everything to play for and while it hadn't been one of the best halves of cup final football ever staged at Hampden, it was nonetheless entertaining.

Much of the second-half action was centred in midfield with minimum goalmouth action. Tommy Wilson did manage to redirect the play with an almighty charge down the right flank, but Thomson just managed to apply his size tens to boot clear.

Mayhem in the United goalmouth in the 61st minute.

Saints forced a corner with Billy Abercromby's flag kick causing consternation in the Tannadice defence. Kenny McDowall tried to apply the finishing touch, but Thomson again made the save.

Campbell Money was the Buddies man of the moment when the Paisley defence left him exposed, but the keeper was on his toes to bring off a fantastic save.

St Mirren were now upping the pressure and McGarvey was unlucky with a drive that ricocheted off Clark's boot.

United did have the ball in the net, but Kenny Hope ensured eternal gratitude from all the Saints fans when he disallowed it for offside.

Time for change and it was a poignant moment in the 77th minute when Ian Cameron took over from McDowall.

Cameron had spent the Saturday morning at Glasgow University taking an exam for his MA degree course. The university hierarchy wouldn't change the date, but did provide some help by rescheduling the exam to start at 8.30 am finishing three hours later - not the best of cup final preparations.

Eleven minutes later the man the whole of Paisley wanted to see appeared with the iconic Tony Fitzpatrick taking over from Paul Lambert.

Into extra time and the break came in the 112th minute when Ian Ferguson took a pass from Brian Hamilton, powered his way past the no nonsense John Holt and pinged a beauty just inside Thomson's right hand post. One-nil to Saints and the whole of Paisley breathed a collective sigh of relief when referee Hope blew the final whistle.

St Mirren had the outstanding player on the field in Neil Cooper with the Hampden media giving him the Man of the Match accolade and crowning him 'Mr Superfit.' And so back to Paisley to celebrate.

Teams:

St Mirren: *Money, Wilson, D. Hamilton, Abercromby, Winnie, Cooper, McGarvey, Ferguson, McDowall (Cameron), B. Hamilton and Lambert (Fitzpatrick).*

Dundee United: *Thomson, Holt, Malpas, McInally, Clark, Narey, Ferguson, Bowman, Bannon, Sturrock (Gallacher) and Redford (Hegarty).*

Referee: *Kenny Hope (Clarkston).*

Attendance: *51,782.*

Campbell Money

**ST MIRREN 0 UNIVERSIDAD OF MEXICO 0
(SAINTS WIN 5-3 ON PENS)**

The Epson Trophy Tournament

28th May 1987

 NOT one classic game, but four all tightly packaged into the Epson Trophy Tournament which immediately succeeded Saints' 1-0 win over Dundee United in the 1987 Scottish Cup Final at Hampden Park.

Having disposed of the Tannadice team thanks to that Ian Ferguson extra time winner, the Saints playing staff and management embarked on a 24-hour jollification spree to celebrate their third Scottish Cup success.

The St Mirren squad had earlier accepted the invitation to compete in this Epson tourney in the Far East, but never in their wildest dreams could they have come to terms with taking part as Scotland's cup holders.

The icing on this soccer cake was the location of the tournament to be staged in the Singapore National Stadium.

So, 24 hours after Billy Abercromby had held the Scottish Cup aloft, the St Mirren party took off from Glasgow Airport - no doubt with some anxious trepidation regarding the energy-sapping 14 hour flight.

One of the cup final stars, Paul Lambert, did not travel to Singapore.

He was allowed to stay behind for family reasons while his team mates continued their celebrations in the glorious Malaysian sunshine.

Also missing from the party was Tony Fitzpatrick who had come on as a sub at Hampden for 17-year-old Paul Lambert.

The 31-year-old Fitzpatrick was given permission by manager Alex Smith to miss out on the Singapore trip to spend a relaxing holiday in Sardinia with his wife and family.

Fitzpatrick had probably not returned to his competitive best after the horrific injury he sustained in a league game against Motherwell at Fir Park.

A double fracture of his jaw had seen the Buddies icon sidelined for the best part of six months, with manager Smith anxious to ensure his playmaker would be in pristine condition for the start of the new season.

The Epson Tournament teams comprised Southampton, Universidad of Mexico and Azzurri of Perth, Australia, in addition to St Mirren.

The teams played each other once with the top two teams in this round robin format contesting the final.

St Mirren's first opponents were the Mexican team who could boast the services of four international players in their line up.

The modus operandi in terms of tactics was totally adverse to those experienced in the Scottish climes.

The Singapore temperatures soared on a daily basis to 90 degrees Fahrenheit so any blistering speedy attacks were kept to a minimum.

The St Mirren line up had Brian Gallagher, back after his leg break, with this University match being his first outing after several months. New boy Keith Walker also made his St Mirren debut.

Out injured were Frank McGarvey and Derek Hamilton, but Peter Godfrey, who missed out on the cup final, returned.

St Mirren also brought in John Butler, another talented youngster, with 17-year-old Norrie McWhirter coming on for Gallagher in the second half.

Goals became something if a rarity as Saints drew 0-0 with the Mexican University followed by a similar scoreline after another gruelling 90 minutes with Southampton.

Just 24 hours later the Buddies faced the Italian side Azzuri from Perth, Australia.

St Mirren suffered an early set back when they fell behind to a scrambled goal, but two great strikes came from Kenny McDowall after the pace of Frank McGarvey and Gallagher had unsettled the Aussie team.

Saints had qualified for the final and would face the Universidad of Mexico, who had put paid to the tournament aspirations of Southampton.

St Mirren went on to win a penalty shoot out 5-3 after 120 minutes of goal-less play. Crucial to the shootout was keeper Campbell Money, who was right on the spot to help St Mirren win the magnificent Epson Cup.

The Scottish Cup holders keeper converted a crucial penalty against the tough Mexican side to help bring more silverware back to Love Street.

The Universidad team didn't do themselves any favours when they had a player sent off for an outrageous tackle on McDowall.

Tempers became further frayed as the Mexican side continued to be overly heavy in the tackle and a skirmish between several players ended with McDowall, the man with a collection of affectionate nicknames such as the 'Mad Monk' and 'Kojak,' receiving a yellow card.

In extra time, the University team adopted a series of time-wasting tactics; however, St Mirren kept their cool - difficult in the sweltering conditions - to outclass the over robust Mexicans.

Billy Abercromby, the Saints outstanding captain, netted the first penalty followed by Peter Godfrey and McDowall before Money converted the fourth to put St Mirren in the driving seat.

Then 17-year-old John Butler, a highly-impressive player, slammed home number five to send the celebrating Saints home with a stylish win.

Butler had deputised for the injured Ferguson in the second half while Walker came on for Gallagher, also an injury victim. Smith was a delighted manager to take the trophy home only days after the Scottish Cup triumph.

Team:

St Mirren: Money, Wilson, Winnie, Abercromby, Godfrey, Cooper, B. Hamilton, Walker, McDowall, Gallagher and Ferguson. Substitutes: Butler and McWhirter.

Kenny McDowall

RANGERS 0 ST MIRREN 1

Premier League

12th August 1989

UST check out the tail end of season 1988-89.

Rangers had won the first Premier League title of their epic nine-in-a-row run and now the Ibrox club, having qualified for the European Champions Cup, were champing at the bit awaiting the German giants Bayern Munich in the first round.

Manager Graeme Souness had populated the Light Blue side with a galaxy of quality players from over the border, recruiting the likes of Terry Butcher, Chris Woods, Gary Stevens, Trevor Steven, Ray Wilkins, Mark Walters - all English internationalists.

As far as the St Mirren player pool was concerned Tony Fitzpatrick's pre-season recruiting drive had principally homed in on Fraser Wishart.

The Johnstone-born Fir Park full-back was signed on a freedom of contract deal.

Manager Fitzpatrick had offered Motherwell £150,000,

but their team chief, Tommy McLean, knocked back the St Mirren offer.

He wanted at least double that amount with the fee being eventually determined via a tribunal.

Further added spice in this opening day fixture was the Rangers debut of one Maurice Johnston, the striker who pronounced the Ibrox club was the only one he had ever wished to play for.

With the 1-0 scoreline posted at 4.45pm in favour of St Mirren it was Graeme Souness who made the pronouncement, 'It's going to be tough at the top.' Rarely can he have spoken a truer word.

The St Mirren fans fully endorsed the Ibrox manager's sorrow as they went out of their way to become party poopers and spoil the flag waving celebrations.

As well as Mo Johnston's competitive debut it was also an occasion for the Light Blue legions to run the rule over Trevor Steven to assess if the former Everton man would shine as the latest jewel in the Ibrox crown.

This was St Mirren's first win at Ibrox since 1980, although they did log in two 1-1 draws at the Govan ground in the 1983-84 campaign.

Even if the 29th minute winner could have sparked of a blazing row, it certainly didn't prevent the Paisley people from celebrating in some style.

That the Rangers strike force had to operate on a diet of meagre rations was largely due to the defensive efforts of their three central defenders Peter Godfrey, David Winnie and Brian Martin.

They were simply superb and were ably backed by keeper Campbell Money who, late in the game especially, racked up a series of spectacular saves as the shots showered in.

It all turned sweet for Saints and sour for Rangers in the 29th minute as not only did Rangers lose a goal that cost them the two points, they also lost their keeper Woods.

And the so-called villain in the eyes of the Ibrox faithful was the effervescent, gritty output generated by Saints' McDowall after Robert Dawson had set up the goal with a cross from the right.

McDowall has enjoyed a fair sackful of nicknames, 'The Mad Monk'; 'Kojak' and 'Clipboard Kenny' to name but a few, but on this occasion the travelling fans were happy to dub him 'King Kenny.'

As the ball zoomed in McDowall challenged Woods at the near post and as the ball broke he bundled it over the line. Woods, meanwhile, crashed to the ground holding his right shoulder.

The blue-laced verbals emanating from the Ibrox stands were protesting more about the McDowall challenge on Woods rather than the loss of a goal.

However, the collision had been caught on camera with the one-on-one confrontation being deemed to be perfectly legal.

After some three minutes of treatment it became clear Woods was not going to make it and former St Mirren star Ian Ferguson took over in goal, while clansman Derek Ferguson moved into the midfield.

The playing format in these days only allowed clubs to field three substitutes and the preferred selection deemed that outfield players were more likely to be subject to injury as opposed to goalkeepers.

Fortunately, the substitute keeper wasn't over troubled between the sticks other than from a well-struck drive from Saints sub Paul Lambert that hit the bar and dropped over.

While the Ibrox feelings were hurt - this wasn't written into the script for their flag unfurling party day - they did take the play to Saints.

However, it must be realised that St Mirren were without a trio of their big name signings in Roddy Manley, Wishart and Tom Black, plus the fact that Paul Kinnaird was suspended.

One man who revved up the applause from the St Mirren fans was new Icelander signing Gudmundur Torfason, before he tired and was eventually replaced by Paul Chalmers.

He did set the Butcher alarm bells ringing when he

diddled the Englishman, created some space and blasted a drive in to the side net.

Teams:

Rangers: *Woods (I. Ferguson), Stevens, Gough, Butcher, Munro, Steven, I. Ferguson (D. Ferguson), Wilkins, Walters, Johnston and McCoist (Drinkell).*

St Mirren: *Money, Dawson, Wilson, Walker, Godfrey, Winnie, Martin, McDowall, Torfason (Chalmers), Davies (Lambert) and Weir.*

Referee: *Donald McVicar (Carluke).*

Attendance: *39,951.*

Gunni Torfason

CELTIC 0 ST MIRREN 3

Premier League

7th April 1990

THE pre-amble to this match at Parkhead hadn't generated any great feel-good factor in and around either the Celts, or Buddies camps.

The previous week Celtic had tripped up at Ibrox with Rangers inflicting an almighty 3-0 thumping on their Glasgow rivals.

St Mirren weren't quite so bad, but an uninspiring 0-0 draw to Motherwell at Love Street didn't generate the anticipated yards of confidence.

Polish striker Jacki Dziekanowski, who failed to make any impression on that Ibrox game, was likely to be replaced by 20-year-old Gerry Creaney.

As for Saints, they were flirting with relegation being just three points ahead of the bottom club Dundee with just five games to go.

Indeed, their prime need was the ability to stick the ball in the net. They had gone seven games without scoring, their last counter being a Kenny McDowall strike against, at Love Street, back in January.

Some hope for Saints revolved around Gunni Torfason.

The big Icelander had sustained a cracked rib and had been out of action for a month. He was fit to play, but was facing a race against time to build up his fitness factor for the trip to Parkhead.

One further crumb of attacking comfort was the anticipated return of Saints other overseas star the West German Thomas Stickroth.

The headlines in the Sunday press said it all - SAINT-SATIONAL !

'Magnificent,' was how St Mirren's beaming boss Tony Fitzpatrick summed up his players performance.

He had watched his side romp to their greatest victory of the season as they completely outclassed Celtic on their home patch.

St Mirren not only gave the denizens of Parkhead lessons on how to distribute the ball in midfield, they also re-discovered the apparent lost art of depositing the ball in the onion bag.

By the 17th minute St Mirren were already looking dangerous. The young Celtic centre half Steve McCahill lost his bearings and mis-headed a clearance that fell kindly for Paul Kinnaird.

The speedy winger demonstrated his sharpness to gather the ball and fire in a drive that rebounded off the upright with keeper Pat Bonner clutching thin air.

Those of a green and white persuasion knew they were fortunate to escape going one down.

Seven minutes later came one of the goals of the season. Stickroth went careering down the right wing to the corner flag, rounded Dariusz Wdowczyk, no easy feat in itself, and flighted an immaculate cross on to Torfason's cranium with the Icelander placing his powerful header well out of keeper Pat Bonner's reach.

If St Mirren's first goal was born out of sheer soccer skill, the second came from the same stable as Anton Rogan's bizarre handball howler at Ibrox the previous week.

With George Shaw lurking in full view, defender Steve McCahill inexplicably rolled the ball into his path.

Shaw then avoided Bonner's desperate dive to give himself the luxury of caressing the ball into the empty net. Sexy soccer eh?

Shaw spontaneously ran to the Celtic fans to celebrate and was immediately booked for his exertions - the only yellow card of the match.

If anyone expected a Celtic comeback they were disappointed. The Parkhead troops were totally dejected and disintegrated as Saints took complete control of the game. In truth, St Mirren threatened every time they went up field.

That threat became a reality in the 64th minute when Paul Lambert wove his way along the 18-yard line, evading the entire Celtic defence and from the edge of the box powered a drive inside Bonner's left hand post.

It was now 3-0 with the home crowd having had enough, their numbers now being considerably reduced at a fast rate of knots.

Now five points ahead of Dundee with four matches to play, manager Fitzpatrick put all thoughts of relegation behind him and looked forward to next season.

It was Torfason who neatly summed it up.

He said, 'That was our easiest win of the season and we haven't won very many. Celtic are going through a bad patch and they never really threatened us.'

Postscript: Dundee were in fact relegated with St Mirren six points ahead of the Dens Park side while Celtic finished fifth.

Teams:

Celtic: *Bonner, Morris, Wdowczyk, Galloway, McCahill, Whyte, Grant, McStay, Walker (Elliot), Coyne and Miller (Creaney).*

St Mirren: *Money, Wishart, Black, Lambert, Godfrey, Manley, Shaw, Martin, Stickroth, Torfason (McDowall) and Kinnaird. Sub not used: Winnie.*

Attendance: *18,481.*

Stuart Taylor

ST MIRREN 1 RANGERS 0

Challenge Match

14th August 1995

NY former player or fan returning to have a look see at St Mirren Park after, say, a 50-year absence might well rub their eyes in disbelief.

One such returning icon was centre forward Alex Crowe whose last match in black and white was in March 1952.

He found it difficult to take in the transformation. Certainly the main stand hadn't changed much over the years, but seats had now been installed in the North Bank with the oval ends of yesteryear's ground now sliced off to provide a rectangular playing arena.

While the Love Street terracing still provided some standing area, a board decision had been taken to upgrade the Greenock Road end of the ground as health and safety requirements now prevented the use of that end of the stadium.

From the phoenix-like ashes of the crumbling Greenock

Road end, with some considerable financial assistance from the Football Trust, a new 3,000 all-seater stand arose to grace the Love Street skyline.

The stand housed more than just 3,000 seats. There was plenty of disabled accommodation on the outside with the internal layout providing two full size five-a-side halls with adequate changing facilities and a gymnasium well utilised by the playing staff.

The venerable Tom 'Tiny' Wharton, he who refereed Saints' 1962 Scottish Cup final with Rangers and was now the deputy chairman of the Football Trust, performed the official opening of this new Caledonia Stand on April 4th 1995.

However, while the new stand was up and running, 3,000 posteriors hadn't as yet adorned the plastic seating and that was accomplished on Monday August 14th 1995, when Rangers were invited to a challenge match with the Phoenix Honda Trophy up for grabs. The silverware had been generously donated by Phoenix Honda chairman John McGuire.

Two days earlier St Mirren's league season had opened with an away fixture to Clydebank at New Kilbowie Park. The 1-1 draw was the first opening day point that the Buddies had gleaned in a five-year stretch.

Unfortunately, club captain Norrie McWhirter wouldn't make the challenge match as he was stretchered off with an ankle and knee injury sustained from a ferocious tackle by James Grady, for which the Paisley-born striker received a straight red.

While the Paisley Daily Express ran a competition to determine a name for the new edifice, the resultant poll came down heavily in support of the Caledonia Stand. Somehow over the years the 'West' or 'Away' stand seemed to grow in popularity.

It was a tremendous Stuart Taylor goal 12 minutes from time that gave Saints custody of the magnificent Phoenix Honda Trophy.

Saints gave as good as they got in the first half.

The Ibrox side might have scored an early goal when Lee Dair lobbed the out rushing Alan Combe, but Robert Dawson managed back to clear.

Long range efforts from Stevie Watson, Ricky Gillies and Taylor all went close while Paul Gascoigne had a couple of off- target headers.

Rangers' Craig Moore was booked for a heavy challenge on Gillies on the 40 minute mark and then right on half time Alex Bone and Brian Reid were also yellow carded by referee Willie Young after they clashed.

St Mirren started the second period with David Elliot replacing Bobby Law and his pace began to trouble Rangers.

The new sub shot wide on 47 minutes with a Gillies drive being blocked by Moore two minutes later.

Then, with 50 minutes on the clock, Rangers' Renfrew boy Iain Nicolson replaced Reid while St Mirren brought on Brian Hetherston for Grant Inglis five minutes later.

Taylor fired a drive into the side netting as the Buddies upped the pace before John Boyd put Elliot in the clear, but he elected to shoot when a cut back to either Bone or Hetherston might have been a more profitable option.

Further changes saw Rangers take off Stephen Wright and Paul Gascoigne for teenagers Steven Boyack and Brian McGinty.

Boyack nearly broke the deadlock in the 73rd minute when he turned an Ian Durrant cross onto the bar, but Jim Dick was on hand to clear. A minute later keeper Combe produced a save of the highest quality to deny Durrant.

Then came that stunning Taylor goal leaving St Mirren to endure a typical Rangers fight back over the final 10 minutes.

Dair shot across the goal with only Combe to beat, but St Mirren were now determined to see the up-for-grabs trophy nestling in the Love Street boardroom and when Combe plucked a Gordon Petric header out of the air with just five minutes remaining you sensed it was not going to be the champions' night.

Saints boss, Jimmy Bone, said, 'It was a good win, but it means nothing since we didn't get three points for it.'

Postscript: Interesting to note the St Mirren contacts, past and future, in the Rangers line up with former Love Street favourite Billy Thomson in goal while Nicolson and Brian McGinty would make their presence felt in future St Mirren team selections.

Teams:

St Mirren: *Combe, Dawson, Dick, Inglis (Heatherston), Watson, McLaughlin, Law (Elliot), Taylor, Gillies, Bone (McGrotty) and Boyd (Smith). Substitute not used: Reserve keeper Money.*

Rangers: *Thomson, Wright (McGinty), Brown (Robertson), Petric, Moore, Reid (Nicolson), Cleland, Gascoigne (Boyack), Durrant, Dair and Mikhailitchenko. Substitutes not used: Wilson and reserve keeper Scott.*

Referee: *Mr W.G.S.Young (Clarkston).*

Attendance: *5,500.*

Hugh Murray

STIRLING ALBION 0   ST MIRREN 1

Scottish League First Division
2nd May 1998

HIS was a game that Sir Alex Ferguson might well have described in his modern day parlance as a 'squeaky bum' affair, whereas Kevin Drinkell, the Albion manager, opted for some more harmonious sounding phraseology in labelling the proceedings as a relegation crunch game.

The second last league game of the season had taken on the mantle of a winner-takes-all encounter with the loser having to plan such away days to the likes of Forfar, Dumfries, Inverness, Alloa and Arbroath in the next season's Second Division.

So how had this demise for Saints in particular come about?

The mid-season table had seen St Mirren sheltering in a relative mid-table comfort zone. League leaders Dundee were out in front being chased by Raith Rovers and Hamilton with little or no possibility of Saints catching them.

But come the Spring, and April in particular, results began to turn nasty.

A couple of 2-2 draws with the attendant dropping of four points came the Paisley way at Ayr United and Hamilton. Then Morton claimed the Renfrewshire bragging rights with a 2-0 result at Cappielow with Raith Rovers and Airdrie dishing the dirty on us, both recording clean sheets at our expense.

The Forthbank side had recorded an even more disastrous run of results and, up until this match with St Mirren, had only logged in two wins from their last seven games and hitting the net on only three outings.

Clearly Stirling goals were at a premium.

A crowd of 2,606 turned up for the battle at the Forthbank Stadium with brilliant sunshine and a temperature to match what was doubtless on offer in Majorca.

Manager Tony Fitzpatrick's team selection saw Alan Combe replacing Derek Scrimgour in goal while Mark Yardley and Andy Roddie were sidelined on the bench, their former starting places going to Junior Mendes and Steven McGarry.

Stirling Albion had one former familiar Saints face in their line up with full back Andy Paterson pulling on their red and white having joined the 'Binos' in August 1994.

A further intriguing statistic on offer prior to kick off was the fact that St Mirren had yet to beat Stirling in the current league campaign with a mere defeat and two draws to their credit.

Just down the road there had been a bit of a dust up back in 1314 at Bannockburn, the local home team putting the English to the sword.

Here at Forthbank the home side were eager to replicate their forefathers' deeds of glory.

They made no secret in that they were on the field for a battle with five Albion players yellow carded inside the first 47 minutes.

But Saints overcame the brawn in the second period and totally steam-rollered the luckless 'Binos.'

Gallons of perspiration were discarded in the heat of the Stirling arena, but it was Hugh Murray who provided all the inspiration.

He had posted his intentions with a header that cannoned off the bar in the first few minutes of the game. But he clearly bettered that effort in the 56th minute.

Taking a measured pass from the diminutive Tom Brown, he pinged a glorious rocket into the postage stamp top corner from the edge of the box.

That strike sparked of a mini pitch invasion by the ecstatic Saints fans.

It brought them abject relief; it brought Murray a yellow card for his over the top celebrations.

Saints were safe and it was Stirling who plummeted down to the Second Division, but the looks on the faces of Fitzpatrick and coach Joe Hughes in the dressing room after the final whistle spoke volumes of their relief at the outcome.

Speaking after the game, Fitzpatrick said, 'It is a disaster that one of us has to go down.

'It's a disgrace that teams like us, who have gone full time to try to improve, are in a small-sized league with two of them facing relegation.'

Stirling Albion's manager, Kevin Drinkell, mirrored his disappointment and commented, 'I am unhappy with the meagre support from the Stirling environs.

'Although we were promoted two years ago, it seems they are content to see us as a Second Division team, however that is not how the 500 loyal supporters who turn up would see it.'

In the Albion boardroom after the game, directors Peter Gardiner and John Smith (Alex's brother) were ashen-faced.

All conversation was totally muted in similar circumstances to a wake - which in reality it was.

With the pressure off, St Mirren went on to win their last match at Love Street taking the scalp of champions Dundee thanks to a Tom Brown goal.

Manager Fitzpatrick took the opportunity to give first

team starts to David McNamee, Chris Kerr and Alan Prentice while Paul Rudden made his debut from the subs bench.

Teams:

Stirling Albion: *McGeown, Paterson, Forrest, Tait, Carberry (Lorimer), Lumsden, Thomas (Hartarsson), Nilsen, Price (Zahana-oni), Bain and Gibson.*

St Mirren: *Combe, Smith, McLaughlin, McWhirter, Fenwick, Winnie, McGarry, Turner, Brown, Mendes and Murray. Substitutes not used: Yardley, Roddie and Watson.*

Referee: *Douglas Smith.*

Tom Hendrie

MORTON 1   ST MIRREN 4

Bell's Scottish League First Division

6th November 1999

ORTON v St Mirren and it doesn't matter if it's a League match, a League Cup game, a Scottish Cup joust or even the Renfrewshire Cup Final, these games are always embellished with hostility which encompasses hatred, malevolence, rancour, animosity and profound verbal abuse.

And why?

Nobody to the author's satisfaction has ever come up with the reason for all the red-blooded violation.

Billy Stark, a St Mirren icon, and at one time the manager of Morton had a simple explanation.

He was convinced it's simply to assume the top dog position in the Renfrewshire local community. Stark went on to say it was right to be passionate about the game and boy, it does provide a tremendous vocal atmosphere.

Prior to this game St Mirren had convincingly knocked over Dunfermline at Love Street and the manner of the execution generated column inches of press speculation and allegation that the Saints manager Tom Hendrie, the former Edinburgh maths teacher, was after the managerial seat at East End Park.

Hendrie was quick to allay any fears.

He said,

- *'There is no substance in the story.'*
- *'I am not applying for the Dunfermline job.'*
- *'I am not touting myself for the job.'*
- *'I have not been approached by Dunfermline.'*
- *'I have a continuing job to do here with St Mirren.'*

Good and bad news was on offer prior to this Renfrewshire derby game.

The bad news was St Mirren had scored just one goal in their last five visits to Cappielow Park - Stephen McGarry's match-winning effort in 19th September 1998 being the last.

The good news was Barry Lavety had scored every time he played in Greenock for Saints - four games, four goals, four wins.

The comforting appraisal of the League table saw Saints out in front on the 27 point mark, while Morton were domiciled on the second bottom slot with 12.

Almost the length of the First Division table separated these sides at the start of the game. By the finish, the difference was the width of the Clyde estuary as the Buddies turned on the style.

In truth, they could have won 8-1 such was the gulf between the sides.

Morton made the early running but St Mirren struck in their first attack in 10 minutes. Barry McLaughlin's forward ball found Junior Mendes. He linked with Iain Nicolson and the wing-back's low cross was turned in from three yards by Sergei Baltacha for his first goal for the senior Saints side.

Controversy arrived on the 27 minute mark as McLaughlin went down following some shoving inside the St Mirren penalty area.

The stand side linesman had his flag up, referee George Clyde consulted him then red-carded Andy Millen for striking the Saints centre back. Yes, you've read the report correctly, the same benign Andy Millen who went on to greater things with St Mirren.

The Buddies pressed trying to make their extra man count but in 31 minutes there was more controversy.

Morton youngster Stephen Whalen broke away, McLaughlin chased back, over hauled the striker then both fell over the edge of the St Mirren box.

Referee Clyde galloped up and immediately red-carded McLaughlin for a 'last man' foul. The TV reruns were, however later to show that Whalen had in fact clearly fouled the big Saints centre back. Imagine the decibel ratings from both sets of fans!

Saints put the blow behind them and in 34 minutes they doubled their advantage. The goal was simplicity itself.

A Nicolson free kick into the box, a nod on by Mark Yardley and there was Lavety to score his tenth goal of the season and continue his remarkable goal scoring run at Cappielow.

'Basher' picked up a knock hereabouts and was replaced by football's 'Mr Tom Thumb' alias the diminutive Tom Brown.

St Mirren looked capable of scoring every time they attacked with Harry Curran clearing off the line and Ally Maxwell pulling off a world class save to deny Baltacha.

But St Mirren did score again just on the interval. Tommy Turner found Yardley who skinned Paul Fenwick and was off in a twinkle toe run to crash home his 50th St Mirren goal.

Morton had a crumb of comfort when David Murie's cross and Warren Hawke's lay off allowed Curran to score from 20 yards in the 48th minute.

Two minutes later St Mirren should have added to their tally.

Scott Walker went rampaging into the box to be decked by Murie, but Maxwell saved Yardley's weak penalty.

Then on the hour mark came the goal of the game if not of the season.

Walker cleared from his own penalty area to Yardley and sprinted up field to take the return pass. 'Scotty' then found Hugh Murray and kept going to get his head to Murray's cross and complete a 90 yard run with goal number four.

Four goals, a local derby, three points and eight points clear at the top and playing good football - the St Mirren fans went home happy.

After Match Postscripts from the red card referee George Clyde: He said, 'There were definite fisticuffs between Millen and McLaughlin that warranted a red card for Andy. As for the McLaughlin and Whalen fracas, I got it wrong and was suitably told off after the game by the referee supervisor. You do try to do your best!'

Teams:

Morton: *Maxwell, Murie (J. Anderson), Morrison, Fenwick, D. Anderson, Matheson, Millen, Curran, Tweedie (Wright), Whalen and Hawke. Substitute not used : McPherson.*

St Mirren: *Roy, McLaughlin, Turner, Walker, Nicolson (Rudden), Murray, Baltacha, Ross, Lavety (Brown), Yardley and Mendes (McGarry).*

Referee: *George Clyde.*

Attendance: *3,733.*

Mark Yardley

ST MIRREN 3   RAITH ROVERS 0

Division One

29th April 2000

OU would have to admit the number of league championship honours that have been ferried St Mirren's way in their 109 league campaigns have been meagre in the extreme.

That patriarch of the sports journalism fraternity and master of the ready quip, Willie Hunter, neatly summed up the lack of Saints silverware.

He commented, 'Whatever other sins are laid at Paisley's front door greed is not among them.'

Willie always had a leaning towards Love Street and once confided his most memorable Saints day wasn't garlanded in silverware, but the afternoon he was introduced to the St Mirren goal machine that was Alex Linwood. Both humble men.

So would the millennium season contribute to the title drought?

Back in 1999-2000 it was one of those re-adjustment seasons for the Scottish Leagues.

Two promotion places were on offer from the First Division with St Mirren's nearest rival being Dunfermline in the final run in.

There had been a few jitters in the Paisley camp when St Mirren lost 2-0 to The Pars at Love Street at the beginning of March.

However, since that set back, the Buddies went on a six game unbeaten run and so arrived at Somerset Park to take on Ayr United to at least clinch promotion if not the actual title.

A crowd of near 5,000 turned up on a day when the Somerset Park PA announcer was regularly taken to the cleaners by the Saints fans who sent a succession of requests asking for the likes of Davie Lapsley, Peter Godfrey and other former Saints to report to the stadium front door after the game.

The first half was goal-less and four minutes into the second period a Junior Mendes goal settled the Paisley nerves.

However, Paisley nails started to be gnawed again when only four minutes later David Craig scored an Ayr equaliser.

It was in the dying seconds of the game that the fleet footed Irishman Paul McKnight skipped through the Somerset Park defence to crack in the winner.

The away section of the terracing went ballistic, Saints were up but on that same day Dunfermline kept in the hunt with a 2-1 win at Inverness.

One thing about winning titles, they become that wee bit tastier if the deed is achieved at home.

So the scene was set for the visit of Raith Rovers on the last Saturday in April.

The local constabulary flexed a muscle or two and demanded the match be all ticket such was the anticipated thirst for success.

The travelling away support from Kirkcaldy was less than

interested - they only wanted 300 tickets.

Not only was the title up for grabs, but also the match heralded the opening of the newly finished Love Street east stand.

Lord McFarlane, chairman of Bell's the Scottish League Sponsors, duly cut the obligatory tape and announced the Paisley Daily Express Stand was open for business.

Love Street was awash with black and white flags and bunting and, as the new stand was formally opened, a thousand helium-filled black and white balloons cascaded into the heavens probably much to the discomfort of the Air Traffic Control lads at nearby Glasgow Airport.

The first half was pretty tense. A first goal would be crucial and neither side was willing to surrender the initiative.

Manager Tom Hendrie re-adjusted his line up and brought on Ian Ross in place of Paul Rudden.

A familiar face appeared in the Stark's Park line up.

Brian Hetherston, affectionately known as 'Bubbles' in his time at Love Street, had drifted eastwards to resurrect his flagging career, but his impetuousness and flavoured verbals cost him dear and was red-carded in the 69th minute.

Clearly some Hendrie verbals of a different hue worked well after the half time break.

Six minutes into the second period Iain Nicolson hoisted over a corner. Ross went for it, but failed to connect. Mark Yardley didn't hang about and the big man lashed home his 19th goal of the season.

Four minutes later Hugh Murray raced down the right flank and when he reached the bye-line sent over a peach of a cross that Steven McGarry deftly head flicked past Guido Van de Kamp.

The resultant celebratory cartwheel demonstrated a substantial increase in the McGarry gymnastic training.

But there was more!

Another three minutes and Saints won another corner.

Ross piloted in a beauty and Barry McLaughlin's cranium

sent the ball spinning into the net. Cue bedlam with the prostrate Mr McLaughlin's well being in grave danger as his team mates piled into the human pyramid.

It was Campbell Money who somewhat unkindly forecast at the turn of the year that the St Mirren bubble would eventually burst.

The First Division champions took it on the chin and emerged from the dressing room for their lap of honour sporting white T-shirts which proclaimed *'THE BUBBLE DIDNAE BURST.'*

Teams:

St Mirren: *Roy, Turner, McLaughlin, Walker, Nicolson (Robinson), Murray, Gillies, Mendes (Lavety), Rudden (Ross), McGarry and Yardley.*

Raith Rovers: *Van de Kamp, McEwan, Andrews, Browne, McCulloch, Tosh, Javary (Clark), Burns, Hetherston, Owusu and Dargo (Stein).*

Referee: *George Clyde.*

Attendance: *8,386.*

MATCH OF THE DAY

Andy Millen

ST MIRREN 2   HAMILTON 1

Scottish League Challenge Cup Final

6th November 2005

ONE would have to admit that St Mirren and the Scottish League Challenge Cup haven't been the best of bedfellows over the years.

The competition was first inaugurated in 1990-91, entitled the Centenary Cup, which was initiated to celebrate the 100th birthday of the Scottish League.

St Mirren's initial entry into the tournament came in the 1992-93 season exiting at a fast rate in the first round thanks to a 2-1 turnover at the hands of Ayr United at Somerset Park.

Hopes were high the following year that some silverware might be gleaned in meeting Falkirk in the final at Motherwell's Fir Park

However, the St Mirren fans literally drew the short straw when they were allocated the open terracing that is now the Davie Cooper Stand and somebody forgot to tell the weather man that torrential rain was a no-no requirement on such cup final days.

The Paisley fans were drenched to the skin and their waterlogged and bedraggled apparel wasn't helped by having the kick off put back by some 15 minutes.

Somebody had miscalculated the fact that when St Mirren reach the final of any cup the Black and White legions turn out in force and so exiting the M74 for Motherwell created a substantial bottle neck.

The players in the dressing room were a mite fractious with Saints skipper on the day, Neil Orr, champing at the bit to get started.

In truth, they never really started on the pitch. Falkirk were too good on the day courtesy of a 3-0 scoreline.

Fast forward 11 years.

Over the period St Mirren had collected an ignominious batch of 1st and 2nd round exits, although they did reach the semi-final in 2002-03. Would 2005-06 be different? It was.

Again remembering the St Mirren fans support for a cup final, considerable dismay was rife when Airdrie United's Excelsior Stadium was the Scottish Football League's preferred venue for the clash with Hamilton.

Would they never learn?

The journey en masse along the M8 by both sets of fans would surely cause a traffic blockage. It did, with the kick off been held back for something bordering on 30 minutes.

Manager Gus MacPherson had taken the team away overnight to a Bellshill hotel to calm their nerves, but having come out to warm up and then back inside followed by another re-entry for a second warm up and back in again, clearly the nerve cells were pretty taut.

Eventually, referee Stuart Dougal got rid of the helium-filled red, black white balloon explosion and blew for the green light.

Accies keeper Dave McEwan was the Douglas Park saviour in the early stages parrying shots on goal from John Sutton and Kirk Broadfoot.

The breakthrough came in the 22nd minute. A consortium of eager free kick takers saw Andy Millen exercise his authority and banished Broadfoot and Simon Lappin for action nearer the Accies goal territory.

McEwan managed to get a hand to the 30-yarder with the

ball breaking to Broadfoot whose pile driver was deflected onto the cross bar.

Lappin was the grateful recipient of the rebound and stroked the loose ball into the far corner of the net. Yes, 1-0 Saints!

Over the years, Hamilton have been doughty opponents for Saints and they came out supercharged after a half time verbal lashing from manage Billy Reid.

Only two minutes after the Bovril break keeper Chris Smith brought off a great save from Brian Carrigan but couldn't prevent Scott Tunbridge slotting home the rebound. One a piece!

It was a ding-dong cup-tie with the silverware destination only being finalised 10 minutes from time.

David van Zanten had a tussle to retain possession, but regained his composure to loft in a superb cross that John Sutton netted with a powerful header. Now it was 2-1 Saints!

Despite the travelling difficulties a magnificent 9,612 crowd took in the game, which contributed to the highest ever attendance recorded at the Excelsior Stadium.

Two interesting portions of trivia from the game...

Operating in the back four for Accies was one Stuart Balmer. He had a circuitous tour of five English clubs after leaving Celtic as a 20-year-old in 1990 and, after playing service with Clyde and Hamilton, he joined St Mirren as first team coach in 2006.

That Peter Pan of Scottish football, the 40-year-young Andy Millen, created history in the final by winning his third Challenge Cup final winners medal having previously been successful with Hamilton in 1991 and 1992.

Teams:

St Mirren: *Smith, van Zanten, Millen (Reilly), Potter, Broadfoot, Murray, Adam (Mehmet), McGowne, Lappin, Kean and Sutton. Subs not used: Reid, Corcoran and Hinchcliffe.*

Hamilton: *McEwan, Thompson, Balmer (Robertson), McLaughlin, Tunbridge, Wilson, Neil, McKenzie, Fleming, Jones (Carrigan) and Keogh (Gilhaney). Subs not used: Brown, Ferguson and Jellema*

Referee: *Stuart Dougal.*

Stewart Kean

ROSS COUNTY 0 ST MIRREN 2

Division One

8th April 2006

THE date is April 1st, that date in the calendar when a cornucopia of practical jokes is inflicted on one's nearest and dearest.

Of more interest to St Mirren was the fact that they could clinch the First Division title - if they could beat Hamilton Accies at Love Street and their nearest rivals St Johnstone and Ross County failed to respectively beat Stranraer and Queen of the South.

It was certainly an All Fools Day!

Saints lost 2-0 to the Accies, St Johnstone won 3-2, while Ross County could only draw 0-0, at Palmerston Park, and lost virtually all title pretensions with another goal-less draw in midweek against Dundee.

Four games to go and St Mirren were still eight points ahead of St Johnstone.

A win up in Dingwall - with the Perth Saints succumbing to Brechin City - would hand the Buddies the title.

Alas it wasn't to be as the McDiarmid Park side won 2-0 at Glebe Park.

That trip up most of the A9 has to be meticulously planned for a stress free excursion.

The team bus would leave Renfrew's Glynhill Hotel at 9.00 am going on to pick up most of the players at 9.30 at the Crow Wood Hotel on the outskirts of Glasgow.

Andy Millen would join the coach further up the A80 at Cumbernauld's Little Chef restaurant then the team coach would go on to the Perth Broxden roundabout for 10.30 stopping to pick up Kevin McGowne, Billy Mehmet and John Potter.

Lunch was scheduled for high noon at the Coylumbridge Hotel, near Aviemore, with the opportunity to stretch one's legs.

Indeed, when Tony Fitzpatrick was the Saints manager he used to walk the team from the hotel into Aviemore to loosen up.

The journey then traversed the Highlands, passing Inverness to arrive at Victoria Park at 1.45 pm. Gus MacPherson was always adamant for a 1.45 arrival at all away games.

Saints had some pre-match fitness problems.

Ian Maxwell, Hugh Murray, Charlie Adam and Simon Lappin were all classified as doubtful after the Hamilton game.

However, Murray, Lappin and Adam were reckoned to be fit for the fray after physio treatment from Karen Aston - but Maxwell was sidelined.

The Ross County administration also had problems.

The club officials were mindful of the expected Paisley invasion for this crunch game and promptly made the away terracing, and the away section of the main stand, all ticket as 1,500 Paisley Buddies were expected.

Manager MacPherson made three changes to the starting line up from the side that lost to Hamilton seven days earlier.

Back into the midfield came the maturity of Millen in

place of Mark Reilly while Stewart Kean replaced Mehmet to partner John Sutton up front.

Midfielder Murray had shrugged off an ankle injury and replaced Iain Anderson.

St Mirren were dealt a bitter blow as early as the eighth minute.

Kirk Broadfoot picked up a bad ankle injury and St Mirren's defensive kingpin had to be replaced by Alan Reid.

County were the livelier team in the early stages, but it was St Mirren who took the lead in the 16th minute with a beauty.

Lappin picked up a loose ball out on the left flank and whipped a cross into the danger zone where Kean was on hand to glance a diving header past the giant County keeper Ian McCaldon.

In the later stages of the first half, keeper Tony Bullock earned his stripes first with a magnificent clearance from Don Cowie, followed almost immediately by smothering a drive from the same County player.

Again the big Saints keeper was on call, this time to keep his charge intact by denying a shot on target from Sean Higgins.

Ross County were forced to make a change at the interval when keeper McCaldon was injured, couldn't continue and had to be replaced by young goalie Joe Malin.

Into the second period and St Mirren forced two quick corners after a prolonged period of pressure, but on both occasions it was Lionel Djebi-Zadi who managed to boot clear.

St Mirren effectively sealed the match in the 63rd minute.

Reid picked out Adam on the left wing with a superb pass. He beelined for the bye-line and launched a cross to the far post where Sutton produced a great downward header, which the young keeper Malin allowed to squirm from his grasp and totter over the line.

Saints went for number three and Lappin flighted a cross over which Potter met with a powerful header, but alas it was a way off target.

Keeper Tony Bullock confided that St Mirren's sensational win felt more like a home game with the might of Paisley vocalising their support immediately behind him.

The Saints stopper put in a performance to match the huge away support with the win eliminating Ross County from the title race.

Return journeys from Dingwall can be pretty dreary occasions - especially if you've failed to pick up the full quota of points.

Equally so, most of the journey is covered in depressing darkness, but this was April, summer time had arrived and that return trip was celebrated in daylight with not only three points in the bag, but virtually the First Division title.

Man of the Match: It could have gone to keeper Tony Bullock, but for sprinting up and down that left touchline and for supplying that peach of a cross for Kean's opener the vote went to Lappin.

Teams:

Ross County: *McCaldon (Malin), Cowan, Djebi-Zadi, Lauchlan, Webb, McCulloch (Anderson), Rankin, Burke (Winters), Higgins, Cowie and McKinlay. Substitutes not used: MacDonald and Tiernan .*

St Mirren: *Bullock, van Zanten, Broadfoot (Reid), Millen, McGowne, Potter, Murray (Anderson), Adam, Sutton (Mehmet), Kean and Lappin. Substitutes not used: Smith and Reilly.*

Referee: *Eddie Smith.*

Attendance: *3,588.*

John Sutton

MOTHERWELL 2   ST MIRREN 3

Scottish Premier League

12th May 2007

OP billing at the tail end of the 2006-07 league campaign wasn't accorded to the top placements.

Celtic were long time home and dry, having taken the title by a 12-point margin from Rangers, no, it was the basement areas, which had developed into a rip-roaring relegation battle.

Regretfully, St Mirren were in a starring role.

At the end of April, with three games to go, the position of the relegation protagonists had Motherwell on 37 points, St Mirren with 30 and Dunfermline one point behind on 29.

Saints then headed for Tannadice on the Saturday and lowered the Dundee United colours by a 2-0 margin, thanks to strikes from Hugh Murray and Kirk Broadfoot while Stewart Kean even had the luxury of missing penalty. Clearly the nerve ends were twanging.

Motherwell then travelled to East End Park on the

following Monday evening to take on Dunfermline and blew the relegation dogfight wide open by losing 4-1 to The Pars. (Note: For PARS read Plymouth Argyle Rosyth Supporters).

By now with only two games to go a blanket of five points covered the bottom three. The penultimate round of games saw Dunfermline travelling to Inverness with Saints taking on Motherwell at Fir Park.

To maximise as much support as possible, particularly for themselves, and generate a full house atmosphere, Motherwell slashed the admission prices to £5 a head with concessions rated at £1.

The initial exchanges were understandably nervy with Motherwell demonstrating a higher degree of composure.

There were 38 minutes on the clock when the claret and amber clan broke the deadlock.

Paul Keegan crossed from his left beat, Kevin McBride headed across the face of the goal and the prolific Ross McCormack nodded neatly past Saints keeper Chris Smith.

The Paisley hearts were a fluttering.

The pendulum was swinging away from Saints and it became worse right at the start of the second half.

Keeper Smith did well to palm over a McBride drive for a corner, but from the resultant flag kick, Andy Millen was deemed to have handled and McCormack made no mistake with the spot kick.

McCormack nearly had a hat trick, but his audacious chip was palmed over by the back pedalling Smith.

Call it a tactical masterstroke, an inspired substitution or whatever you like, but it was manager Gus MacPherson who called the shots by replacing Alex Burke and Millen with John Sutton and Billy Mehmet.

A total of 54 minutes had been played, with plenty of time to alter the pattern of the game.

That alteration took only two minutes.

First a fairly innocuous header from sub Sutton was allowed to slip through keeper Colin Meldrum's legs. And three minutes later fellow sub Mehmet curled a beauty into the net after Broadfoot had set him up.

Panic in the Fir Park ranks, the pendulum had swung in a different direction.

BBC trackside pundit, Chick Young, was going bananas on the touchline.

Through his earphones he had heard that Dunfermline were 2-1 down at Inverness and he was jumping up and down like a demented puppet on a string. Was there more to come?

There was - plenty!

In the closing stages, Sutton saw a header tipped onto the bar then six minutes from time the Paisley Battalions went ballistic. And Sutton became the hero of the hour as he rifled home the priceless winner.

Hugs and kisses all round - and that was only the St Mirren directors!

The Motherwell hierarchy was less than chuffed.

The results had partially gone their way and, along with St Mirren and that result in Inverness, both were safe.

St Mirren decidedly milked their SPL survival for all it was worth after producing a Lazarus-like comeback.

But the Motherwell fans created a Lanarkshire version of a ticker tape parade with Fir Park littered with season ticket books at the final whistle disgruntled fans throwing them on the pitch.

Indeed, there was widespread condemnation of manager Maurice Malpas's leadership and with that post match demonstration it was felt his jacket could be on the proverbial shaky peg.

MacPherson offered some post match thoughts on his substitutions.

He said, 'I was right to start with Sutton and Mehmet on the bench.

'I've always been honest with the players and Kean and Burke did well last week up at Tannadice. They had every right to start but it didn't work for them today.

'The way the team responded was an indication of the character we've spoken about all season.'

It was an anti-climax for the last round of the league games.

Motherwell went up to Tannadice to draw 0-0 with Dundee United, Dunfermline went 3-0 down at home to Falkirk while St Mirren lost 1-0 to their perennial problem team Inverness Caley Thistle.

Teams:

Motherwell: *Meldrum, Corrigan, Craigan, Kinniburgh, Quinn, McBride, Fitzpatrick, Vadocz, McGarry (McLean), McCormick and Keegan (Clarkson). Substitutes not used: Graeme Smith, Kerr, Darren Smith, Connolly and Murphy.*

St Mirren: *Smith, van Zanten, Potter, Broadfoot, Maxwell, Corcoran, Murray, Millen (Sutton 54), Reid, Kean and Burke (Mehmet). Substitutes not used: Hinchcliffe, Brady, Mackay, McKenna and McGinn.*

Referee: *Mike Tumilty.*

Attendance: *9,277.*

Stephen McGinn

ST MIRREN 1   RANGERS 0

Premier League

5th October 2008

NY time the fixture list programmes an imminent match against Rangers, and realising the expected quality of the Ibrox side, it is highly desirable to have your full complement of players available for selection.

So, prior to this televised Sunday match with the Light Blues, it was understandable that manager Gus MacPherson should be somewhat incandescent at St Mirren's previous match with Motherwell at Fir Park .

The MacPherson rant centred upon a red card given to Franco Miranda for an alleged elbowing offence against former Saint John Sutton. Referee Willie Collum didn't see the incident and it was down to the eagle-eyed linesman to indicate that Franco should walk.

A further galling factor was John Sutton's post match interview stating that the red card was an error of refereeing judgement.

This was St Mirren's third red card of the season and clubs do have the right of appeal to the SFA but such an overture costs £1,000 a time and any appeal by St Mirren would centre round the angles as portrayed by the TV cameras.

Subsequent viewing indicated doubt as to the validity of such an appeal and, having already lost out on a previous appeal, it boiled down to a saving of £1,000 from the petty cash box.

All this plus a defensive headache for the Saints management team as, in addition to Miranda having to sit out the Rangers game, Jack Ross, Will Haining and David Barron were all nursing injuries.

As the day drew near it was an interesting conjecture to anticipate the welcome that former Saints Kirk Broadfoot and Charlie Adam would receive on their return to St Mirren Park.

Another former Saint also making headlines on the back pages was Chris Iwelumo who had been selected for the Scotland World Cup squad to face Norway at Hampden.

As usual, the media pack was happy to extol the fact that the last time St Mirren had beaten Rangers at St Mirren Park was way back on April 1986.

However, the hacks failed to point out that Saints had beaten Rangers twice that season at home.

Not only the Press, but the bookmaking fraternity had it in for Saints. The pre-match odds on a St Mirren win were 10/1, 1/3 for a Rangers victory and 7/2 for a draw.

There was just one change from the St Mirren starting 11 from the side that lost to Motherwell earlier. Both Ross and Haining were deemed fit to play. And it was Haining who replaced the suspended Miranda.

The intensity of the game was mirrored when Pedro Mendes clobbered Dennis Wyness and received a yellow card for his trouble with only seven minutes played.

John Potter was pretty agile in defence, first heading clear a fiercely struck drive from Mendes and then repeating the feat to stop a shot from Adam.

Rangers' striker Kenny Miller was a dangerous customer with his speed. He got the better of Steven Robb and smashed over a dangerous cross, but fortunately there were no takers.

Gary Mason was penalised for a foul on Jean Claude D'Archeville, but no matter which way the Ibrox giants went Saints were matching them in every department.

It wasn't all Light Blue activity. And when Billy Mehmet scampered down the left channel, he sent over a well-struck pass towards Wyness, but the former Caley Thistle man hadn't the legs to accept the offering.

No scoring at the break and on the resumption St Mirren were experiencing some difficulty in getting out of their own half.

Rangers were becoming increasingly desperate to notch that opening goal and St Mirren were equally determined to keep them out.

Rangers midfielder Kevin Thomson took a bad one in a 50-50 challenge and was stretchered off to be replaced by Kyle Lafferty. The Ibrox alarm bells were beginning to jingle with goal predator Kris Boyd replacing D'Archeville.

St Mirren gradually worked their way up field and began to ask questions of the Rangers defence before Stephen McGinn and Craig Dargo replaced Andy Dorman and Dennis Wyness.

On the 74th minute mark cue bedlam for the Saints faithful.

Jack Ross pumped the ball well up field where Billy Mehmet collected and released Stephen McGinn.

Dargo, meanwhile, dragged two back-tracking Ibrox defenders away from the young midfielder who drifted in before smashing an excellent left-foot drive into the far corner of the net from all of 22 yards. Keeper Allan McGregor was not amused .

Rangers upped their work rate, but were stymied once again when Kris Boyd's shot came crashing back of the upright.

Into injury time and Saints keeper Mark Howard stuck out a leg to deny Steven Davis.

The St Mirren rearguard action was then totally epitomised when Kirk Broadfoot powered in a header which was cleared just under the cross bar in a concerted leap by four Saints defenders.

McGinn, who wasn't even born the last time Saints beat Rangers at Love Street, didn't embark on any champagne swigging celebrations - he was only too focused to try and cement his place in the St Mirren line up in the next reserve match against Falkirk 48 hours later.

Teams:

St Mirren: *Howard, Ross, Haining, Potter, Cuthbert, Robb, Dorman (McGinn), Mason, Brady (Murray), Wyness (Dargo) and Mehmet. Substitutes not used: Smith, Hamilton, Brighton and McAusland*

Rangers: *McGregor, Broadfoot, Papac, Weir, Bouhgerra, Thomson (Lafferty), Mendes, Adam, Davis, D'Archeville (Boyd) and Miller. Substitutes not used: Alexander, Beasley, Dailly, Niguez and Loy*

Referee: *Willie Collum.*

Attendance: *7,520.*

Chris Smith

ST MIRREN 1 CELTIC 0

Homecoming Scottish Cup 4th Round
7th March 2009

O appreciate the niceties, the drama and the euphoria of this Scottish Cup tie, one has to indulge in a spot of back-tracking - to season 1961-62 to be precise.

Home in on Monday 26th March with St Mirren playing Celtic at Love Street in a re-arranged league fixture. Nothing went right for the Buddies and they were cuffed 5-0.

Five days later they again faced up to the Hoops in the Scottish Cup semi-final at Ibrox. No doubt the thoughts of the pools punters sensed a good thing with Celtic ringed as a sure fire banker.

But after such a turnover St Mirren were more than anxious to redeem their self esteem and sent the Hoops home to think again on the back of a 3-1 turnover thanks to goals from Donnie Kerrigan, Tottie Beck and, of all people, Willie Fernie - a former mainstay at Parkhead.

So, it had been 47 years since St Mirren had beaten their

Glasgow rivals in the Scottish Cup.

Fast forward then to 2009.

St Mirren are at Celtic Park on league duty and the Gods were unkind. Celtic hitting top form in scoring seven, while Saints hit the skids and registered a big zero.

There were some extenuating circumstances.

Jack Ross received a straight red after only 26 minutes deemed to have denied a goal-scoring opportunity by referee Crawford Allan, contentious in the extreme.

Allied to stemming the green and white flow with 10 men, Saints young custodian, Chris Smith had a nightmare game - taking the blame for a number of the goals while John Potter added to the shambles with a bonny headed own goal.

Aberdeen were due at New St Mirren Park on the following Tuesday, so what would Gus MacPherson do regarding his young keeper?

Answer, he kept him in the team to kick-start his confidence factor and, in truth, apart from a few wayward kicks he turned in an acceptable performance.

But would manager MacPherson retain the Smith goalkeeping services for the cup-tie after his calamitous nadir at Celtic Park seven days earlier?

He did with Smith turning in a match-winning stint that completely erased the previous week's headlines of 'Calamity Chris.'

Composed and combative St Mirren kept this game on a tight rein throughout.

And, crucially, they took full advantage of the chance that Celtic presented them.

Ironically, that came from Shunsuke Nakamura, the previous week's hat trick hero.

The Japanese midfielder attempted to hit a first time pass across the field but only succeeded in playing in Craig Dargo.

The diminutive striker played a quick one-two with Andy Dorman and, racing into the penalty box like a whippet off the leash, he slipped the ball through the legs of Stephen

McManus who responded by illegally chopping down the little striker.

Referee Charlie Richmond pointed to the penalty spot and Billy Mehmet stepped forward to slam home then treat the Paisley fans to that now famous semaphore wiggle goal celebration.

What was ironic was McManus receiving only a yellow card, as the incident was a carbon copy of the Ross foul on Scott McDonald the previous week.

Consistency is a factor seemingly somewhat bereft among the current crop of whistlers.

Celtic keeper Artur Boruc then prevented St Mirren doubling their lead with a fine reaction stop from Dorman while from the rebound there was a borderline challenge from McManus, again on Dargo, which just about sniffed above the legal limits.

Aiden McGeady then upped the Parkhead work rate as time was running out.

His cross saw Jan Vennegoor of Hesselink nod in a header that was just too easy for keeper Smith.

Just three minutes from time the big Dutchman again managed to get his cranium onto a corner from Nakamura but the now confident keeper Smith was more than able for the task.

So, 47 years on and the identical scenario was again being unfolded. There seems to be a consensus of opinion that teams outwith the Old Firm have a cheek to even attempt to de-throne either of the Glasgow giants.

One would remind them it is a level playing field and arrogance doesn't easily fit into the equation.

Post match interviews from the two managers were streets apart in offering crumbs of solace for the waiting press corps.

Celtic's Gordon Strachan, asked where it all went wrong, as if it was a right of those in green and white to automatically progress to the semi-final, was terse in his reply, 'St Mirren.' he answered.

Gus MacPherson, a thoughtful and forensic coach, was

more circumspect in his post match analysis.

He had spared his side the old-school hairdryer treatment, calmly reminded his team of their duties to the club, to the fans and to their own professional pride. He wanted a reaction, he got it and was delighted to be only one game away from the cup final.

Teams:

St Mirren: *Smith, Ross, Potter, Haining, Camera, Dorman, Murray, Thomson, Brady, Mehmet and Dargo (Wyness). Substitutes not used: Howard, Hamilton. Barron and McGinn.*

Celtic: *Boruc, Hinkel, Caldwell, McManus, O'Dea (Conroy), Nakamura, Crosas (Samaras), Scott Brown, McGeady, McDonald and Vennegoor of Hesselink. Substitutes not used: Mark Brown, Hartley and Loovens.*

Referee: *Charlie Richmond.*

Attendance: *5,925.*

Billy Mehmet

ST MIRREN 1 HEART OF MIDLOTHIAN 0

CIS League Cup semi-final

2nd February 2010

T won't have escaped those with black and white blood in their veins that St Mirren's relationships with the latter stages of the League Cup tournament have been sparse in the extreme.

Since the competition was inaugurated in season 1946-47 Saints contribution to the database has seen the Buddies contest only one final and that in the 1955-56 campaign losing out 2-1 to Aberdeen.

The back up at the semi-final stage has been equally bereft with only three appearances, the last being in February 2001 when a certain Gus MacPherson was in the opposition patrolling Kilmarnock's right backbeat.

Now those with bus pass potential might take umbrage at the three semi final appearances claiming there was yet another one.

True and not true. The League Cup competition

originated during the Second World War years in 1940-41 when the Scottish Cup tourney was suspended with the participants being limited to the central belt clubs.

Saints did reach the first ever semi final in 1940-41 only to be beaten 4-1 by Rangers at Hampden.

How many can rhyme off the St Mirren line up on that occasion? Try Johnstone, Savage, Craven, Cox, McDowall, Kelly, Caskie, Brady, Linwood, McPhail and Deakin - memories, memories.

But back to the 2010 campaign.

Initially Saints semi with Hearts was destined for Hampden Park, but with the likelihood of an attendance of around 10,000 it was deemed more practical, from an atmospheric point of view, to stage the tie at Motherwell's Fir Park Stadium.

The last time St Mirren had contested a cup tie at Fir Park was the 1993 Challenge Cup Final against Falkirk with Saints missing out on a 3-0 scoreline.

On that occasion the kick off had to be knocked back by 15 minutes to allow the travelling Paisley support to wind their way off the M74.

The weather was abysmal with torrential rain of stair rod proportions and turning the Fir Park sward into a quagmire.

Would the Motherwell pitch be in a more playable condition than that 1993 day? The answer was an emphatic no!

The Fir Park surface had been transformed into a series of turf carpet tiles as the Motherwell ground staff had tried to provide a positive playing surface.

Regretfully many of the turf tiles failed to knit with man-size divots appearing all over the pitch.

Even Saints manager MacPherson was out on the pitch during play to stamp down numerous turf clods.

And Hugh Murray even had the indignity of tripping over a raised dollop of turf!

St Mirren had disposed of East Stirlingshire, Ayr United, Kilmarnock and Motherwell in the previous rounds, while

Hearts had lowered Celtic's silverware aspirations with a sole Michael Stewart penalty at Celtic Park.

Saints opted for a defensive formation with three at the back giving Chris Innes a place alongside John Potter and Lee Mair. The five-man midfield saw Jack Ross and David Barron as rampaging wingbacks.

Saints kicked off towards the massive away stand. Ross was in the mood and a series of charging right wing runs saw a clutch of quick fire crosses homing in on keeper Marian Kello who dealt with the blitz in a confident fashion.

Michael Higdon almost made the breakthrough after 13 minutes when a deflected ball landed at his feet but the big striker's feet assumed a 'granny knot' configuration and the chance was lost.

Just on the half hour mark David Barron was penalised for a foul on Ian Black just 30 yards from goal but Paul Gallacher held Michael Stewart's drive with ease.

Early in the second period Hugh Murray was played in by Billy Mehmet, but the midfielder's shot went wide. Mehmet then had a go after some interplay by Steven Thomson and Andy Dorman, but his drive slammed into the side netting.

Saints were growing in stature and made the breakthrough on the 51-minute mark. A quality cross field ball from Ross saw Higdon brilliantly dummy the ball for Mehmet, steaming in like an express train, to power a beauty into Kello's top left hand postage stamp from all of 25 yards.

The travelling Paisley fans went ballistic and nearly lifted the Davie Cooper stand off its foundations.

Three minutes later Saints should have sealed it.

Mehmet eased a pass through to Dorman with the midfielder outstripping the Tynecastle defence only for keeper Kello to make a fantastic block.

Hearts were rocking at this stage, but still had the stamina for some late drives on the St Mirren goal. However, the Paisley rearguard, with John Potter regularly applying cranium to leather, stood firm.

Postscript: Rangers defeated St Johnstone in the other

semi final at Hampden and so set up a cup final date with St Mirren at Hampden on Sunday 21st March 2010.

Teams:

St Mirren: *Gallacher, Ross, Innes, Mair, Potter, Barron, Murray, Dorman (O'Donnell), Thomson, Mehmet and Higdon (Dargo). Substitutes not used: Howard, Brady and Robb.*

Hearts: *Kello, Thomson, Wallace, Jonsson, Bouzid (Kucharski), Zaliukas, Smith (Glen), Black (Santana), Nade, Stewart and Driver. Substitutes not used: Mulrooney and Ridgers.*

Attendance: *9,170.*

Referee: *Charlie Richmond.*

Andy Dorman

ST MIRREN 4   CELTIC 0

Scottish Premier League

24th March 2010

O fully appreciate the theatre of this match, one has to backtrack some 72 hours and the Sunday afternoon CIS League Cup final against Rangers at Hampden Park.

They don't come along that often.

After all, a total of 133 years of competitive cup football in Paisley has seen St Mirren contest only seven national cup finals.

The infrequency generates a high degree of Paisley anticipation and this latest cup final picnic was no exception.

The assembling fans were in a good mood with one avid Paisley punter forking out £10 on a 10-1 wager for Saints to win courtesy of a Billy Mehmet goal.

Manager Gus MacPherson's pre-match aim was to ensure no early goals were conceded and so David Barron was drafted into the back three with five in midfield.

No early goals were lost, in fact almost the reverse, as Saints dominated the match with three corners being posted in first five minutes. And it took the Ibrox club 25 minutes before Paul Gallacher, the Saints custodian, was called on to take care of a Miller drive.

Five minutes from the break Barron unleashed a screamer which had keeper Neil Alexander beaten all ends up only to clip the top of the crossbar.

No scoring at the interval with a St Mirren realisation that this cup was there for the taking.

Midway through the second period came a major flashpoint.

Rangers' Kevin Thomson felt hard done by when John Potter inadvertently clipped his heels. No foul was given with the Ibrox man now on a revenge mission, launching a ferocious tackle on Saints' Steven Thomson.

It became a virtual gathering of Clan Thomson when referee Craig Thomson immediately brandished a straight red for the man in blue.

Worse was to follow for those with light blue affinities. And there were 19 minutes left when Danny Wilson hauled Craig Dargo back for a professional foul just outside the box, a second red and Rangers now down to nine men. The vocal renderings from the Paisley following were now in full flow as visions of that elusive League Cup began to manifest themselves in the St Mirren trophy cabinet.

Attack after attack rained in on the Rangers goal mouth with severe bouts of frustration developing as St Mirren failed to make their superiority count. It's said it is difficult to play against ten men, here it was becoming increasingly difficult to take on nine.

Then tragedy. The 84th minute, a forlorn Rangers break out, three on two with the Saints defence, a cross from Stevie Naismith with a Kenny Miller header beating keeper Gallacher and the silverware was destined for Ibrox.

Never in the history of the League Cup final campaigns has so much energy been expended by so many for so little return. So near and yet so far.

Billy Mehmet was in tears, half the Saints support wept gallons. Saints would never ever have such a cup final opportunity again.

It was almost akin to a death in the family.

Paisley despondency knew no ends. What was there to look forward to on the immediate horizon?

Well, Celtic were due at St Mirren Park three days later. Would MacPherson and Andy Millen be able to lift the morale of the player pool?

MacPherson had further player problems on his plate. Chris Innes was still injured; David Barron had crocked a knee at Hampden and might miss the rest of the season while Graham Carey, on loan from Celtic, couldn't play against his parental club. What followed was the stuff dreams are made of. It was simply Saints-tastic!

St Mirren went with Hampden Man of the Match, Michael Higdon, on the bench leaving Dargo and Mehmet up front.

It was the flying Craig Dargo that posted Saints initial intent with his movement luring Josh Thompson into a lunging tackle which earned him a third minute booking.

St Mirren had a clear penalty shout in the 38th minute when Edson Braafheid barged Dargo on the back, but referee Charlie Richmond was having none of it.

However, the Saints annoyance turned to sheer delight a minute later.

Billy Mehmet linked up with Steven Thomson on the right wing with the ball being swept into the path of Andy Dorman and the Welshman drilled a 20-yarder past the unprotected Lukasz Zaluska.

One up at the break, there was an emerging feeling that a possible upset was on the cards. That feeling assumed euphoric proportions in the 57th minute.

Dargo broke clear, dragging the shaky Thompson wide, before plying a neat one-two with Mehmet. He then played the ball across the box for Steven Thomson to hammer home into the far corner.

Breathtaking stuff but in the words of a certain Irish

comedian - 'there's more'.

Andy Dorman sent the Paisley faithful into a delirious frenzy with a gallop down the left wing in the 83rd minute to fire home numero three past the helpless Zaluska. Had Dorman fluffed that one the energetic Billy Mehmet was also on hand to complete the coup de gras.

Hereabouts Celtic Boss Tony Mowbray had introduced five strikers into his line up and, with winger Aiden McGeady operating at right back, the Celtic game plan was in tatters. No wonder Mowbray was the instant recipient of his P45 the following day.

The Buddies were now on fire with ageing grandparents urging their offspring to securely log these events safely into their memory banks. And these banks were full to overflowing when with four minutes to go Thomson latched onto a pass to fire home Saints' fourth.

By now the Saints support had become ballistic and 'We want five' became their chant then 'Easy, easy' champagned the night air as St Mirren celebrated their biggest win over the Parkhead side since 1959, when the Buddies sent the Hoops home to think again in the wake of the Scottish Cup semi-final at Hampden.

Teams:

St Mirren: *Gallacher, Ross, Mair, Potter, Robb, Thomson, Murray, Brady, Dorman (O'Donnell), Dargo (Loy) and Mehmet (Higdon). Substitutes not used: Howard, McLennan and Devlin.*

Celtic: *Zaluska, Wilson, Thompson, O'Dea, Braafheid (Rasmussen), Samaras, Ki Sung-Yueng (Fortune), N'guemo, McGeady, McGowan and Keane. Substitutes not used: Boruc, Zhi, Crosas, Caddis and Hinkel.*

Referee: *Charlie Richmond.*

Attendance: *5,018.*

SAINTS CLASSIC GAMES CHRONOLOGICALLY LISTED

Hearts 0	St Mirren 3	26th April 1919
St Mirren 2	Notts County 1	20th May 1922
Celtic 0	St Mirren 2	10th April 1926
St Mirren 3	Morton 2	3rd July 1943
St Mirren 1	Rangers 0	10th July 1943
Kilmarnock 1	St Mirren 5	5th April 1947
St Mirren 7	Queen ot South 1	6th September 1947
St Mirren 6	Morton 1	24th August 1948
St Mirren 5	Hearts 5	18th August 1951
Queen ot South 2	St Mirren 7	11th September 1954
Aberdeen 2	St Mirren 1	22nd October 1955
Partick Thistle 1	St Mirren 5	11th February 1957
Hibernian 5	St Mirren 5	22nd February 1958
St Mirren 2	Hibernian 1	22nd November 1958
St Mirren 10	Peebles Rovers 0	13th February 1959
Celtic 0	St Mirren 4	4th April 1959
St Mirren 3	Aberdeen 1	25th April 1959
St Mirren 15	Glasgow Univ'ty 0	30th January 1960
Third Lanark 0	St Mirren 8	28th February 1961
St Mirren 5	Raith Rovers 1	20th January 1962
Celtic 1	St Mirren 3	31st March 1962
St Mirren 1	Arbroath 1	17th April 1968
St Mirren 4	Berwick Rangers 0	29th April 1968

Dundee 0	St Mirren 4	19th April 1977
St Mirren 1	Liverpool 1 (4-5)	12th December 1977
St Mirren 3	Bristol City 1	16th April 1980
Elfsborg 1	St Mirren 2	17th September 1980
Celtic 1	St Mirren 2	22nd November 1980
St Mirren 1	Aberdeen 1	3rd January 1981
Airdrieonians 3	St Mirren 4	5th September 1981
St Mirren 4	Morton 3	10th March 1984
St Mirren 3	Slavia Prague 0	2nd October 1985
Hammarby 3	St Mirren 3	23rd October 1985
St Mirren 1	Hammarby 2	6th November 1985
St Mirren 2	Hearts 1	11th April 1987
St Mirren 1	Dundee United 0	16th May 1987
St Mirren 0 (5-3)	Univ'ad of Mexico 0	28th May 1987
Rangers 0	St Mirren 1	12th August 1989
Celtic 0	St Mirren 3	7th April 1990
St Mirren 1	Rangers 0	14th August 1995
Stirling Albion 0	St Mirren 1	2nd May 1998
Morton 1	St Mirren 4	6th November 1999
St Mirren 3	Raith Rovers 0	29th April 2000
St Mirren 2	Hamilton 1	6th November 2005
Ross County 0	St Mirren 2	8th April 2006
Motherwell 2	St Mirren 3	12th May 2007
St Mirren 1	Rangers 0	5th October 2008
St Mirren 1	Celtic 0	7th March 2009
St Mirren 1	Hearts 0	2nd February 2010
St Mirren 4	Celtic 0	24th March 2010